WJEC CBAC

Students' Book

GCSE English / English Literature

Roger Lane

Consultants
Barry Childs
Ken Elliott
Margaret Graham
Stuart Sage
Ted Snell
Ken Welsh

imagine   EXPLORE
prose   review   media
describe   DRAMA   analyse
persuade   poetry

OXFORD
UNIVERSITY PRESS

OXFORD
UNIVERSITY PRESS

Great Clarendon Street, Oxford OX2 6DP

Oxford University Press is a department of the University of Oxford.
It furthers the University's objective of excellence in research, scholarship,
and education by publishing worldwide in

Oxford New York

Auckland Bangkok Buenos Aires
Cape Town Chennai Dar es Salaam Delhi Hong Kong Istanbul
Karachi Kolkata Kuala Lumpur Madrid Melbourne Mexico City Mumbai
Nairobi São Paulo Shanghai Taipei Tokyo Toronto

Oxford is a registered trade mark of Oxford University Press
in the UK and in certain other countries

British Library Cataloguing in Publication Data available

ISBN 0 19 831884 7

10 9 8 7 6 5 4 3

Typeset by Mike Brain Graphic Design Limited, Oxford

Printed in Italy by Rotolito Lombarda

Acknowledgements
The Publisher would like to thank the following for permission to reproduce
photographs:

Alamy Images: p 41; Biffa Waste Services Ltd: p 85; Matin Bond: p 107;
Corbis: p 152; Corbis/Randy Duchaine: p 45; Corbis/Martin Withers, Frank Lane
Picture Agency: p 157; Corbis/Ed Kashi: p 83 (bottom); Corbis/Stephanie Maze:
p 83 (top); Corbis/Jennie Woodcock, Reflections Photolibrary: p 51;
Corbis/Peter Turnley: p 159; Corel Professional Photos: pp 11, 12, 47, 87, 120
(both); Empics/John Walton: p 78; Mary Evans Picture Library: p 140;
Getty Images: p 54; Hulton Getty: pp 9, 25, 27, 31; Illustrated London News:
20 (both); NASA: p 92; Oxford University Press: pp 53, 72 (both), 108;
Photodisc: p 70; Rex Features: p 97; Rex Features/Paul Brown: p 68;
Rex Features/Andrew Dunsmore: p 89; Rex Features/Stephen Meddle: p 69;
Rex Features/Ray Tang: p 57;

Illustration (p 153) by Paul Hunt

Cover photograph by Digital Vision

We are grateful for permission to include the following copyright material in this
book:
Mark Ainsbury: extract from 'Can't Take My Eyes Off Baku … ' copyright ©
Mark Ainsbury December 2002, first published on *http:www.cardiffcity-mad.co.uk/news*, reprinted by permission of the author.
***W.H. Auden:** 'Song' from *As I Walked Out One Evening* edited by Edward
Mendelson (Faber and Faber, 1995), reprinted by permission of the publisher.
Beryl Bainbridge: Extract from *Young Adolf* (Gerald Duckworth & Co. Ltd,
1978), reprinted by permission of the publishers.
Bruce Chatwin: extract from *On the Black Hill* (Jonathan Cape, 1982), reprinted
by permission of the Random House Group Ltd.
Iain Crichton Smith: extract from *Consider the Lilies* (Victor Gollancz, 1968),
reprinted by permission of the Orion Publishing Group Ltd.
Stella Gibbons: Extract from *Cold Comfort Farm* (Lawrence and Wishart,
2002), copyright © Stella Gibbons 1932, reprinted by permission of Curtis
Brown Ltd, London on behalf of the Estate of Stella Gibbons.
Susan Hill: extract from *The Woman in Black* (Vintage), copyright © Susan Hill
1983, reprinted by permission of Sheil Land Associates.
John Idris Jones: 'Laugharne Castle' from *Say That Again* edited by Mairwen
Jones and John Spark (Gomer Press, 1997), reprinted by permission of the
author.
****Katherine Mansfield:** extract from *The Voyage*.
***George Orwell:** extract from *Nineteen Eighty-Four* (Secker & Warburg, 1949),
reprinted by permission of A.M. Heath Company Ltd.
Sheenagh Pugh: 'Cameraman' from *Selected Poems* (Seren, 1990), reprinted
by permission of the publisher.
Bob Thomas: extract from 'Astronauts Mark 30th Anniversary of Last Moon
Landing' first published *Houston Chronicle* 1999, reprinted by permission of the
Associated Press.
Dylan Thomas: extract from 'Extraordinary Little Cough' from *Portrait of the
Artist as a Young Dog* (Dent, 1940), reprinted by permission of David Higham
Associates Ltd.
Dylan Thomas: extract from *Under Milk Wood* (J.M. Dent, 1975) copyright ©
J.M. Dent 1975, reprinted by permission of David Higham Associates Ltd.
***Robert Tressell:** extract from *The Ragged Trousered Philanthropists* (Grant
Richards Ltd, 1914).
Keith Waterhouse: extract from *Billy Liar* (Penguin, 1962), reprinted by
permission of David Higham Associates Ltd.
Evelyn Waugh: Extract from *Decline and Fall* (Chapman, 1928), copyright ©
Evelyn Waugh 1928, reprinted by permission of PFD on behalf of the Evelyn
Waugh Trust.
***Nigel Williamson:** extract from 'Mick Jagger, Popstar – My Best Teacher' first
published in *Times Educational Supplement*.
***Jeanette Winterson:** extract from *Oranges Are Not The Only Fruit* (Pandora
Press, 1985).
Also:
*Extract and illustration from 'P Plates' first published in *Drive On* magazine
2002.
*Extract from 'Young Britons Quizzed Over State of the Planet' first published on
http://portal.telegraph.co.uk 09.10.02.
Extract and illustration from 'At the Heart of the World's Greatest Marathon
FLORA' first published on *www.london-marathon.co.uk*, (London Marathon Ltd
Publications, 2002), reprinted by permission of the publisher.
Outline information regarding the video 'What Happened on the Moon' An
investigation into Apollo taken from www.aulis.com, with permission.
****'What is teaching like?' taken from the website of the Teaching Training
Agency, www.canteach.gov.uk.
'Wild Welsh Water' as it appears on *Brecon Carreg* labels (for the time being),
reprinted by permission of Spadel UK.
*Extract from entry for 'Water' from *Hutchinson Softback Encyclopedia* (1991).

Although we have tried to trace and contact copyright holders before
publication, in some cases this has not been possible. If notified we will be
pleased to rectify any errors or omissions at the earliest opportunity.

Contents

To the student

This book is made up of 19 units that take you through the sorts of text and question you are likely to meet in the GCSE English and English Literature exams. The units are grouped into five sections, each one covering a type of reading or writing, and at the beginning of each section is a summary of what you will be tested for.

Throughout, the book focuses on the skills that you need to get the highest grades you can in the exams. It should work whether you are expecting to take Foundation Tier papers or Higher Tier papers because there is a common structure to the WJEC exams and, of course, a common need for everyone to improve reading and writing skills. The book should take away the myths and the mysteries of English exams and help you to believe that anything is possible.

So, whether you are aged 16+ or 60+, give it a go! Good luck!

Roger Lane

ROGER LANE

Author's acknowledgements

Thanks to all of the consultants, whose collective wisdom of GCSE English and English Literature I hope I have properly represented.

Thanks to all the teachers who helped in the development of this book, especially those who turned up at focus groups on wet nights after school.

Thanks to Elizabeth Evans for research and original writing.

Thanks to Karl Mearing for administrative support.

Dedication

This book is dedicated to Arthur Parker – on behalf of teachers of GCSE English in Wales and England.

Using the units

Each section of the book specifically targets an area of the final exams, as described on each opening page. The grid on the right shows how the units might be used to support students in the English and English Literature exams.

GCSE COMPONENT	UNITS
ENGLISH PAPER 1 SECTION A: Reading (English literary heritage)	1.1 – 1.4
ENGLISH PAPER 1 SECTION B: Writing (Descriptive and imaginative)	2.1 – 2.3
ENGLISH PAPER 2 SECTION A: Reading (Non-fiction and media)	3.1 – 3.4
ENGLISH PAPER 2 SECTION B: Writing (Transactional and discursive)	4.1 – 4.3
ENGLISH LITERATURE PAPER (Specification A)	5.1 – 5.4 (also 1.1 – 1.4)
ENGLISH LITERATURE PAPER (Specification B)	5.1 – 5.5 (also 1.1 – 1.4)

The skills and texts needed for coursework are covered in the WJEC *Coursework Guide*, also published by Oxford University Press. Parts of this book, however, will be useful to students when preparing written and oral coursework, and these are listed in the grid on the right.

GCSE COMPONENT	UNITS
COURSEWORK: Reading / English literature	1.1 – 1.4 5.1 – 5.5
COURSEWORK: Writing to *inform, explain, describe* Writing to *explore, imagine, entertain*	2.1 – 2.3
COURSEWORK: Writing to *argue, persuade, advise* Writing to *analyse, review, comment*	4.1 – 4.3
COURSEWORK: Speaking and listening (Group discussion/interaction)	All units adaptable
COURSEWORK: Speaking and listening (Individual contribution)	2.1, 2.2 4.1, 4.2
COURSEWORK: Speaking and listening (Drama-focused activities)	1.4, 5.3

Prose reading

GCSE English Paper 1

Section A (Reading: 15%) will test through structured questions the reading of a prose passage from the English literary heritage by a major writer with a well-established critical reputation.*

Reading and responding in writing to extracts of literary prose is an important part of your work in English. These extracts are generally from narrative fiction texts, such as novels and short stories, and your response to them is central to the way you will be assessed in English and English Literature.

In literature, meaning is communicated through language, narrative voice, plot, setting, character and relationship. In your GCSE work, three main skills are being assessed:

a location and reorganization – your ability to find information and use your own words

b inference – your ability to read 'between the lines'

c appreciation of style – your ability to examine the way the writer writes.

This section of the book contains four units:

1.1 Personal response You will learn how to express your thoughts and feelings about characters and situations.

1.2 Deeper meaning You will learn to dig deeper for the less obvious meanings and the bigger ideas in a text.

1.3 How does the writer ... ? You will look closely at the skills and techniques used by writers.

1.4 Empathy You will learn about examining the role of a given character and trying to understand their motives and behaviour.

* The text extracts in this section have been chosen with this definition in mind. However, there will always be disagreements about the critical reputation of writers. The choices made here, therefore, might not all be approved for 'live' exam papers. Nevertheless, these extracts do successfully target and assess the appropriate reading skills necessary for the exam.

Unit 1.1 Personal response

All of the following typical exam questions require some kind of personal response. Each one of them asks **you** directly for your opinions and encourages you to explore and develop your thoughts and feelings.

> What are **your** thoughts and feelings about the opening of this story?
>
> What are **your** first thoughts and feelings about the meeting between ____ and ____ ?
>
> What do **you** learn about ____ in these lines?
>
> What first impressions do **you** have of ____ and ____ and their relationship?
>
> How effective do **you** find these lines as an ending to the story?
>
> (You should use the extract to support your answers.)

With questions like those above, you can feel confident that what you write, if it is sensible, is unlikely to be wrong. Your views will be respected. You do not have to show any technical knowledge here but you do have to build up a case. In other words, it is not enough to write just one or two sentences. You should try to develop a fairly long paragraph, in keeping with the length of all your answers in the reading and response part of your GCSE exam. You should aim for between half a side and a side of A4 paper (average-size handwriting).

WARNING Do not drift away from the text you are supposed to be reading. Personal response is a test of reading, so you should keep your focus clear. However, do try to use your own words and sentences where possible.

Read the following passage from a short story called *Tickets, Please* by D.H. Lawrence. During the First World War, with many men in the armed forces fighting abroad, all the conductors on the trams were women. Only the drivers and inspectors were men. This short extract describes a young inspector. As you read it, think particularly about the inspector's character.

The inspector's name is John Thomas Raynor – always called John Thomas, except sometimes, in malice, Coddy. His face sets in fury when he is addressed, from a distance, with this abbreviation. There is considerable scandal about John Thomas in half a dozen villages. He flirts with the girl conductors in the morning, and walks out with them in the dark night, when they leave their tram-car at the depot. Of course, the girls quit the service frequently. Then he flirts and walks out with the newcomer: always providing she is sufficiently attractive, and that she will consent to walk. It is remarkable, however, that most of the girls are quite comely, they are all young, and this roving life aboard the car gives them a sailor's dash and recklessness.

Now answer the following question:

🔶 **What are your impressions of John Thomas from these lines?**

To help you, here are a few things you might consider. Even though it is a short text, there is plenty to work on.

🔶 You know the man's name and you know his nickname.
🔶 You know he's a tram inspector, probably in charge of the young women conductors.
🔶 You know he flirts with the girls. (You can use the word flirt as your own, but you should try to extend the idea a little.)
🔶 You might pick up the idea that John Thomas is a bit choosy, that he won't go with just any girl.
🔶 You could offer the opinion that he is a bit of a lad who likes to have a good time.
🔶 BUT what about the words 'malice', 'fury', and 'scandal'?
🔶 And what about the fact that John Thomas is at home working on the trams and not away fighting in the war?

Now read the following passage, which is the opening of *Nineteen Eighty-Four*, a famous futuristic novel by George Orwell. It is not particularly easy to understand with confidence on first reading, so puzzle out the situation cautiously. Winston Smith, the main character in the novel, is entering Victory Mansions, the block of flats in which he lives. Think about the character Winston Smith and the setting Victory Mansions as you read this extract.

It was a bright cold day in April, and the clocks were striking thirteen. Winston Smith, his chin nuzzled into his breast in an effort to escape the vile wind, slipped quickly through the glass doors of Victory Mansions, though not quickly enough to prevent a swirl of gritty dust from entering along with him.

The hallway smelt of boiled cabbage and old rag mats. At one end of it a coloured poster, too large for indoor display, had been tacked to the wall. It depicted simply an enormous face, more than a metre wide: the face of a man of about forty-five, with a heavy black moustache and ruggedly handsome features. Winston made for the stairs. It was no use trying the lift. Even at the best of times it was seldom working, and at present the electric current was cut off during daylight hours. It was part of the economy drive in preparation for Hate Week. The flat was seven flights up, and Winston, who was thirty-nine and had a varicose ulcer above his right ankle, went slowly, resting several times on the way. On each landing, opposite the lift-shaft, the poster with the enormous face gazed from the wall. It was one of those pictures which are so contrived that the eyes follow you about when you move. BIG BROTHER IS WATCHING YOU, the caption beneath it ran.

You may be uncertain about what you have just read, even though the words themselves do not appear to present many difficulties. Often in these situations, something strange is being described and it is not wise to be too hasty in your guesswork. You may have some ideas along the following lines:

- Some of the details are very **strange**. What particularly did you find puzzling?
- The setting is extremely **bleak.** Which details about Winston Smith and Victory Mansions do you find depressing?
- Certain points in the passage are **ominous** or **threatening**. What stands out for you as uncomfortable to imagine?

In the grid below, the key details have been selected and supplied for you in the left-hand column. Copy the grid* and fill in the empty boxes with thoughtful answers. Some of the comment boxes have been filled in with possible responses, which you could add to with thoughts of your own.

EVIDENCE FROM THE TEXT	IDEA	EXPANDED COMMENT
'the clocks were striking thirteen'	Strange	*This is unusual. It could just be the 24-hour clock, but it makes us think right from the start.*
'in an effort to escape the vile wind'	Bleak	
'a swirl of gritty dust'		
'smelt of boiled cabbage and old rag mats'		*It probably turns your stomach and is likely to be a dreadfully sickly and stale smell.*
'an enormous face, more than a metre wide'	Ominous	
'the electric current was cut off during daylight hours'		
'Hate Week'		
'a varicose ulcer'		
'one of those pictures which are so contrived that the eyes follow you about'		
'BIG BROTHER IS WATCHING YOU'		

* Photocopiable masters of all the grids in this book are supplied in the *Teacher's Book.*

1 Prose reading

Now answer the following question:
* **What are your thoughts and feelings about the opening of this story? Organize the best of your details, ideas and comments from your grid into a fluent response.**

The next passage is from the historical novel *Consider the Lilies* by Iain Crichton Smith. In the Scottish Highlands, in the first half of the 19th century, ordinary people were evicted from their homes by rich landowners because it was more profitable for the land to be used for rearing sheep. In this extract, Patrick Sellar, acting for the Duke of Sutherland, arrives on a white horse to visit an elderly widow, to deliver the news that she must leave her home.

He came over to where she was sitting.

Because she had been taught to be courteous and obedient to her superiors she stood up. It wasn't easy, but she succeeded. She was surprised that he didn't tell her to sit down for some of his superiors did this. Some of them even meant it, and had a kind of careless politeness, which this man didn't have.

'Good day to the gentleman,' she said.

She expected him to say 'good day' in return but he only grunted.

'Will the gentleman go in?' she asked.

'All I have to say to you can be said here,' said the man.

But of course that wouldn't do. It wouldn't be polite to keep a stranger outside the house.

She went inside and waited for him to follow her, which he did. At first she felt a little dazed going inside, for the room was dark and slightly chilly after the warmth outside. She sat down on one of the two chairs. She noticed that the stranger didn't want to sit but she signed to him to do so and he sat on the bench, which was close to the door. He kept hitting his whip against the bench and even though this irritated her she didn't ask him to stop. He was, after all, a guest in her house. She waited in silence with her hands crossed for him to begin to speak, staring into the empty grate.

'I suppose you'll know why I'm here,' he began.

And then she had a flash of revelation. Perhaps he had come about her pension. Her husband had been killed in the war in a place called Spain, and now that she came to think of it, he had talked to her once of a man on a white horse.

'It is about the pension?' she asked.

'What pension?' he asked.

'The pension for my man,' she said. 'They said I would get a pension.'

. . .

'I'll tell you what I came for,' said the fat little man thumping the bench with his whip.

She looked up: she had almost forgotten him. And suddenly she saw that his burning little eyes were those of an enemy. She couldn't think why this should be so. She was sure she had never seen him before in her life and she couldn't understand how she had offended him.

'Will the gentleman have a cup of tea?' she said, though that would mean setting and lighting a fire and she was very tired.

'No, I haven't time for tea.'

She didn't wonder why he didn't say 'Thank you' or 'Tapadh leibh' because sometimes they said it and sometimes not. It depended what mood they were in. Anyway, he wouldn't know any Gaelic.

She didn't particularly like the look of him. His head wasn't Highland. It was too heavy and the face was too fat and red, and the eyes in the head were small and burning.

'I came to tell you,' he was saying, 'that you'll have to leave the house.'

Now answer the following question:

❧ **What are your first thoughts and feelings about the meeting between the old woman and Patrick Sellar?**

To help you organize your thoughts, look back at some of the key details about the woman and the man. Build up your understanding of the two people and the way the meeting between them develops.

Choose five details about the woman and five details about the man and comment on them. For example, the woman 'had been taught to be courteous and obedient to her superiors', which suggests that she will behave respectfully in this situation. However, the man's response to the woman ('he only grunted') suggests immediately that his manners are not up to hers – he's blunt and rude.

The grid below contains a number of relevant quotations from the extract for you to consider as you think about the content and structure of your answer. Remember that you should select appropriate material from the text to support your response.

THE WOMAN
'had been taught to be courteous and obedient to her superiors'
'She was surprised that he didn't tell her to sit down'
'She expected him to say "good day" in return'
'It wouldn't be polite to keep a stranger outside'
'she felt a little dazed'
'she noticed that the stranger didn't want to sit'
'even though this [the whip] irritated her she didn't ask him to stop'
'She waited in silence ... staring into the empty grate'
'She had a flash of revelation ... "Is it about the pension?"'
'she had almost forgotten him'
'suddenly she saw that his burning little eyes were those of an enemy'
'She couldn't think why ... and she couldn't understand how she had offended him'
'Will the gentleman have a cup of tea?'
'She didn't wonder why he didn't say "Thank you" or "Tapadh leibh"'
'She didn't particularly like the look of him'

1 Prose reading

THE MAN
'he didn't tell her to sit down'
'[he didn't have] a kind of careless politeness'
'he only grunted'
'All I have to say to you can be said here'
'didn't want to sit'
'He kept hitting his whip against the bench'
'I suppose you'll know why I'm here'
'I'll tell you what I came for'
'he didn't say "Thank you" or "Tapadh leibh"'
'His head wasn't Highland'
'the face was too fat and red'
'the eyes in the head were small and burning'

Finally in this unit, read the following extract from *Oranges Are Not The Only Fruit* by Jeanette Winterson. The young girl, Jeanette, has a strongly religious background. Here, she describes some of her difficulties in fitting in at primary school.

At school I couldn't seem to learn anything or win anything, not even the draw to get out of being dinner monitor. Dinner monitor meant you had to make sure everybody had a plate and that the water jug didn't have bits in it. Dinner monitors got served last and had the smallest portions. I'd been drawn to do it three times running and I got shouted at in class for always smelling of gravy. My clothes were gravy-spotted and my mother made me wear the same gymslip all week because she said there was no point trying to make me look clean as long as I had that duty. Now I was sitting in the shoebags, with liver and onions all down my front. Sometimes I tried to clean it off, but today I was too unhappy. After six weeks' holiday with our church, I'd be even less able to cope with any of it. My mother was right. It was a Breeding Ground. And it wasn't as though I hadn't tried. At first I'd done my very best to fit in and be good. We had been set a project just before we started last autumn, we had to write an essay called 'What I did in my Summer Holidays'. I was anxious to do it well because I knew they thought I couldn't read or anything, not having been to school early enough. I did it slowly in my best handwriting, proud that some of the others could only print. We read them out one by one, then gave them to the teacher. It was all the same, fishing, swimming, picnics, Walt Disney. Thirty-two essays about gardens and frog spawn. I was at the end of the alphabet, and I could hardly wait. The teacher was the kind of woman who wanted her class to be happy. She called us lambs, and told me in particular not to worry if I found anything difficult.

'You'll soon fit in,' she soothed.

I wanted to please her, and trembling with anticipation I started my essay ... 'This holiday I went to Colwyn Bay with our church camp.'

The teacher nodded and smiled.

'It was very hot and Auntie Betty, whose leg was loose anyway, got sunstroke and we thought she might die.'

The teacher began to look a bit worried, but the class perked up.

'But she got better, thanks to my mother who stayed up all night struggling mightily.'

'Is your mother a nurse?' asked the teacher, with quiet sympathy.

'No, she just heals the sick.'

Now answer the following question:
- **What are your impressions of the young girl in this passage?**
Answer this question 'against the clock', as you would in an exam. In other words, write at least half an A4 page in about 15 minutes.

- This time, do not write a full-scale plan or detailed notes, but do track through the evidence of the passage to select your key details.
- Remember to trust your own judgement. Do not leave your best ideas in your head – get them into your written answer.
- Here are a couple of tips to consider with this particular question and passage: YES, the writing is humorous and YES, the girl is out-of-the-ordinary!

Exam tips

- There are no set answers to questions requiring some personal response. Your ideas will be respected and valued if you are clearly responding to the text you have been asked to read. Try to develop your answer beyond one or two sentences, but be sensible with your time – so know when to stop!
- These kinds of question will appear on Foundation and Higher Tier papers. They are questions that test your Reading skills, not your Writing skills.
- For a really successful answer, try to select appropriate material from the text to reach valid, sensible conclusions. The very best answers will select and explore appropriate details from the text. They will have depth and show a real insight and understanding of the text.

Unit 1.2 Deeper meaning

What are the character's thoughts and feelings about what happens in these lines?

How does what happens in these lines change the character?

What do the two characters learn from this experience?

What is the character's attitude to the situation in these lines?

What is going through the character's mind in these lines?

How do the characters behave in these lines?

How does the character see himself/herself in these lines?

(You must refer closely to the text in your answer.)

This unit focuses on questions that particularly give you the opportunity to dig deeper for meaning when you are reading novels and short stories. You should understand from the start that there is no clear line to be drawn between questions that ask directly for personal response and those that do not. Look at the focus of the set of questions above and you will spot that the emphasis is no longer on you the reader, but on the character on the page.

Positioning and key words

Setting yourself in position to answer a question and then looking in the right direction are both so important.

Note the differences between **a** and **b**:

a *Look at lines 1–20*
What are your thoughts and feelings about character X in these lines?

b *Look at lines 21–34*
What are character X's thoughts and feelings in these lines?

Although fairly obvious when pointed out, it is all too easy to start from the wrong spot, face the wrong way, and go down the wrong track!

Finding the deeper meaning in a piece of literature (or reading 'between the lines') is not a precise business. For example, extra understanding in an answer may be partly achieved by simply extending a response to the correct length. BUT – you also need to explain bits of the text clearly in your own words, you need to see the less obvious points and you need to work out on occasions what the writer really meant, that is, what s/he inferred or implied. Ideally, by the end, you would draw out at least one accurate summarizing point about the whole text, a clincher that fits with all the smaller points.

A note on irony

Academics write whole books on irony, so a few lines cannot hope to give you the full picture! Irony is any of the following – subtle meaning, double meaning, shades of meaning, changes of meaning.

Sarcasm (the lowest form of wit?!) deals with meanings that are more or less the OPPOSITE of the truth. The best substitute for sarcasm in writing is 'heavy irony'.

When people use the word 'ironic', they are referring perhaps to a neat, unexpected twist of fate, such as:
'It is ironic that the goal that finally relegated Manchester United was scored by one of their former heroes, Denis Law.'
OR
'It is ironic that Geri Halliwell, the acknowledged leader of the Spice Girls, was the one to leave the group.'

Above all, do not be troubled by the difficulty of understanding irony. Read closely and try to judge the atmosphere, the mood, the tone of what you are reading. Try also to judge where there is a shift or a change in any of those.

Read the following passage from *Tickets, Please* by D.H. Lawrence. As you read it, think particularly about the two characters, Annie and John Thomas.

During the First World War, with many men in the armed forces fighting abroad, all the conductors on the trams were women. Only the drivers and inspectors were men. The following short passage discusses the relationship between Annie, a conductor, and John Thomas, a young inspector.

So Annie walked out with John Thomas, though she kept her own boy dangling in the distance. Some of the tram-girls chose to be huffy. But there, you must take things as you find them, in this life.

There was no mistake about it, Annie liked John Thomas a good deal. She felt so rich and warm in herself whenever he was near. And John Thomas really liked Annie, more than usual …

But with a developing acquaintance there began a developing intimacy. Annie wanted to consider him a person, a man: she wanted to take an intelligent interest in him, and to have an intelligent response. She did not want a mere nocturnal presence, which was what he was so far. And she prided herself that he could not leave her.

Here she made a mistake. John Thomas intended to remain a nocturnal presence; he had no idea of becoming an all-round individual to her. When she started to take an intelligent interest in him and his life and his character, he sheered off. He hated intelligent interest. And he knew that the only way to stop it was to avoid it. The possessive female was aroused in Annie. So he left her.

It is no use saying she was not surprised. She was at first startled, thrown out of her count. For she had been so very sure of holding him. For a while she was staggered, and everything became uncertain to her. Then she wept with fury, indignation, desolation, and misery. Then she had a spasm of despair. And then, when he came, still impudently, on to her car, still familiar, but letting her see by the movement of his head that he had gone away to somebody else for the time being, and was enjoying pastures new, then she determined to have her own back.

1 Prose reading

Now answer the following question (write at least half a side of A4 paper):

◆ **What is Annie's attitude to her relationship with John Thomas?**

This is a question mainly about Annie, but also about John Thomas. The question could easily have been 'What are Annie's thoughts and feelings in these lines?' but the words *attitude* and *relationship* add extra challenges. There is no shortage of things to say about Annie, but how do you give a focused answer? How do you set about answering this question?

Look at the key words:

Attitude – *a way of thinking or feeling about someone or something, typically one that is reflected in a person's behaviour.* Annie's behaviour will be closely linked to her attitude and allow us to work out an overview of her attitude.

Relationship – *the way in which two (or more) people regard and behave towards each other.* We need points about Annie, and her reactions to John Thomas.

Tracking the text – points about Annie

In the grid below, key details have been selected for you on the left. Copy the grid and fill in the empty boxes with thoughtful explanations.

TEXTUAL REFERENCE	EXPLANATION/COMMENT
... walked out with John Thomas, though she kept her own boy dangling in the distance.	*She's hedging her bets, keeping the other lad as a reserve! This might suggest some doubts about John Thomas.*
... liked John Thomas a great deal.	*'A great deal' suggests something a little special*
... wanted to consider him a person, a man ...	
... did not want a mere nocturnal presence ...	
... she prided herself that he could not leave her.	
The possessive female was aroused in Annie.	
... startled, thrown out of her count.	
... she had been so very sure of holding him.	
... she wept with fury, indignation, desolation, and misery.	
... she determined to have her own back.	

Overview – Annie's attitude

A good way of dealing with attitudes is to ask yourself the question – What attitudes are possible in a given situation? Once those are considered it is easier to position yourself in the right area and to develop your ideas carefully. For example – is Annie *casual* and *easy-going* about her relationship or is she *committed* and *serious*?

ATTITUDE?	EXPANSION
Casual or committed?	*She is committed, not at all casual, despite keeping her 'own boy' in tow. She seems to be looking for a full-time relationship.*
Easy-going or serious?	
Positive?	
Proud?	
Emotional?	

When completing the task, use the material gathered in the work you have done so far on this passage. One last tip – you **can** use the contrasting attitude of John Thomas to reinforce points about Annie's attitude, e.g 'In contrast to John Thomas, who only wants a casual relationship, Annie is fully committed ...'

Read the following passage from *Young Adolf* by Beryl Bainbridge. The novel is about an imaginary period in the early life of Adolf Hitler, when he supposedly visited England and stayed in Liverpool as a student and artist with his half-brother Alois. (Alois really did live in Liverpool.)

The young Adolf, who is lazy, outstays his welcome in the family home of Alois and Bridget. In this scene, Alois loses his patience with him.

At first Alois didn't notice that Adolf had taken to the couch again. He thought he was sleeping late and retiring early. He discovered the truth when he returned in the middle of the day to collect some samples he needed. Bridget was at the table giving the baby his dinner. He asked her if Adolf was ill.

'No,' she said. 'I'm sure he's not ill.'

'Is he eating?'

'Like a horse,' she said. It was only because she cooked him food all the time. Actually, she felt Adolf would be quite happy subsisting on a diet of jam butties.

'How long has he been like this?'

'Three days,' she replied truthfully. She understood his point of view. It wasn't fair Adolf lying in state, living off the fat of the land, so to speak, while Alois spent his waking hours wearing out his shoe leather in an attempt to better himself.

Gripping the sleeper roughly by the shoulder, Alois rolled him off the couch and on to the floor. 'I'm not angry,' he shouted, the little veins purple in his cheeks. 'I've no objection to a man lounging about till Kingdom Come if he pleases, so long as it's in his own house and at his own expense. You can pack your bags and go.'

1 Prose reading

'Go,' said Adolf. 'Go where?'

'What the hell is it to me,' fumed Alois. 'Back where you came from. Anywhere you like. You didn't care where I was going all those years ago.'

Adolf made no attempt to rise from his knees. He crouched there clasping and unclasping his hands like a penitent schoolboy. In the time between dreams and hitting the floor his face had lost its look of stupor and acquired a haunted expression.

'You're welcome to the blankets,' cried Alois, picking them off the carpet and throwing them at him. He strode to the hearth and seized hold of the length of bent piping. 'And you can take this bloody work of art with you.'

He hurled the metal with all his strength towards the couch. It skimmed the air a fraction above Adolf's head and struck the wall. Rebounding, it clattered harmlessly to the floor. Alois ran into the adjoining room and slammed the door behind him. The baby, chuckling, waved its fists.

'He might have brained you,' said Bridget, looking severely at Adolf. She left darling Pat in his chair and followed her husband into the bedroom.

'God forgive me,' whispered Alois. 'I could have been up on a murder charge.'

'You missed,' she consoled him. 'He'd try the patience of a saint.'

'Once,' he said, 'when I needed real help he wrote and told me to go hang myself.'

'He never,' she cried. 'You shouldn't give him house room.'

'It was signed in my stepmother's name,' he said. 'But it was in his hand writing.'

She couldn't think how to comfort him. They had grown so far apart. She was ashamed of herself for feeling a little glow of pleasure at his misery.

'I don't know what to do for the best,' Alois said forlornly. He was used to making iron decisions. There was nowhere Adolf could go. He hadn't the price of a tram ticket. He prowled back and forth between the bed and the wardrobe.

Now answer the following question:
* **How do Adolf and Alois behave in this passage? Refer closely to the text in your answer.**

Track as much of the surface detail about the two characters as possible. You could write firstly about Adolf's behaviour and then about Alois's behaviour. You should try to explain what inferences can be made about Adolf, and then what explanations can be made for what Alois does.

Try to include comments on the following:
* Adolf on the couch, sleeping and eating
* Alois arriving home and confronting Adolf
* Adolf's reaction(s) and Alois's violence
* Alois's reflections in the other room.

Remember that you have two characters to write about. You should attempt to select and explore details from the text and make thoughtful, perceptive comments about each character and the relationship between them.

Read the following passage from *On the Black Hill* by Bruce Chatwin. The novel is set in the border area of England and Wales and it follows closely the lives of twins Lewis and Benjamin Jones, born at the start of the 20th century. In this extract, the twins are onlookers at a rally to persuade local men to volunteer for the army. Jim the Rock, their neighbour, figures prominently in this incident.

In the Congregation Hall of Rhulen, a border village, during the winter of 1914–15, the public has gathered to watch a show of filmslides from the war in France and to listen to the local Colonel Bickerton and a visiting Major.

One by one, a sequence of blurred images flashed across the screen – of Tommies in camp, Tommies on parade, Tommies on the Cross-channel ferry; Tommies in a French café, Tommies in trenches, Tommies fixing bayonets, and Tommies 'going over the top'. Some of the slides were so fuzzy it was hard to tell which was the shadow of Miss Isobel's plume, and which were shell-bursts.

The last slide showed an absurd goggle-eyed visage with crows' wings on its upper lip and a whole golden eagle on its helmet.

'That', said the major, 'is your enemy – Kaiser Wilhelm II of Germany.' There were shouts of 'String 'im up' and 'Shoot 'im to bloody bits!' – and the 10 Major, also, sat down.

Colonel Bickerton then eased himself to his feet and apologised for the indisposition of his wife.

His own son, he said, was fighting in Flanders. And after the stirring scenes they'd just witnessed, he hoped there'd be few shirkers in the district.

'When the war is over,' he said, 'there will be two classes of person in this country. There will be those who were qualified to join the Armed Forces and refrained from doing so ... '

'Shame!' shrilled a woman in a blue hat.

20 'I'm the number One!' a young man shouted and stuck up his hand.

But the Colonel raised his cufflinks to the crowd, and the crowd fell silent:

'... and there will be those who were so qualified and came forward to do their duty to their king, their country ... and their womenfolk ... '

'Yes! Yes!' Again the hands arose with fluid grace and, again, the crowd fell silent:

'The last-mentioned class, I need not add, will be the aristocracy of this country – indeed, the only true aristocracy of this country – who, in the evening of their days, will have the consolation of knowing that they have done what 30 England expects of every man: namely, to do his duty ... '

'What about Wales?' A sing-song voice sounded to the right of Miss Bickerton; but Jim was drowned in the general hullabaloo.

Volunteers rushed forward to press their names on the Major. There were shouts of 'Hip! Hip! Hurrah!' Other voices broke into song, 'For they are jolly good fellows ... ' The woman in the blue hat slapped her son over the face, shrieking, 'Oh, yes, you will!' – and a look of a childlike serenity had descended on the Colonel.

He continued, in thrilling tones: 'Now when Lord Kitchener says he needs you, he means YOU. For each one of you brave young fellows is unique and 40 indispensable. A few moments ago, I heard a voice on my left calling, "What about Wales?"'

Suddenly, you could hear a pin drop.

'Believe you me, that cry, "What about Wales?" is a cry that goes straight to my heart. For in my veins Welsh blood and English blood course in equal quantities. And that ... that is why my daughter and I have brought two automobiles here with us this evening. Those of you who wish to enlist in our beloved Herefordshire Regiment may drive with me ... But those of you, loyal Welshmen, who would prefer to join that other, most gallant regiment, the South Wales Borderers, may go with my daughter and Major Llewellyn-Smythe to

50 Brecon ... '

This is how Jim the Rock went to war – for the sake of leaving home, and for a lady with moist red lips and moist hazel-coloured eyes.

Now answer the following question:

♣ **How do the Colonel and the Major try to encourage local men to join the Army?**

When answering this question, you should consider:
♣ what they do
♣ what they say
♣ how they say it.

The bullet points here offer support, suggesting how you might see sections of your answer. However, you might also track the sequence of events in the passage and keep alert to the 'how' as well as the 'what'.

Using a grid like the one below will help. The prompts on the left are short. See what you can do to develop your comments in relation to the key words of the question. Start from the premise that the military want these men to join up and they will use every trick in the book to get their way!

SECTION OF TEXT	FOCUS ON 'TRY TO ENCOURAGE'
Filmslides (lines 1–7)	The still, blurred pictures of the Tommies (British soldiers) in action will make the men in the audience ... Most of the images show the men in training or relaxing, so ...
Appealing to sense of duty (lines 8–24)	Colonel Bickerton really gets going here ... Using the example of his son fighting in Flanders is shrewd, because ...
Welsh patriotism (line 25 – end)	The colonel is quick to backtrack and turn his mistake (forgetting Wales) to his advantage, by ... He builds up the atmosphere ...
Overview of whole passage	They persuade the men by using a number of emotional appeals and tactics ...

Read the following passage from *The Woman in Black* by Susan Hill. In this extract, the first-person narrator of the story, Arthur Kipps, is in the process of being drawn into the mystery of the woman in black. This ghost story is set in the area of Eel Marsh House and the windswept marshes beyond Nine Lives Causeway. The atmosphere of the setting affects the mood of the narrator.

It was the perfect day for bicycling, cold enough to make the wind burn against my cheeks as I went, bright and clear enough for me to be able to see a long way in all directions across that flat, open landscape.

I intended to cycle to the next village, where I hoped to find another country inn and enjoy some bread and cheese and beer for lunch but, as I reached the last of the houses, I could not resist the urge that was so extraordinarily strong within me to stop and look, not westwards, where I might see farms and fields and the distant roofs of a village, but east. And there they lay, those glittering, beckoning, silver marshes with the sky pale at the horizon where it reached down to the water of the estuary. A thin breeze blew off them with salt on its breath. Even from as far away as this I could hear the mysterious silence, and once again the haunting, strange beauty of it all aroused a response deep within me. I could not run away from that place, I would have to go back to it, not now, but soon. I had fallen under some sort of spell of the kind that certain places exude and it drew me, my imaginings, my longings, my curiosity, my whole spirit, towards itself.

For a long time, I looked and looked and recognized what was happening to me. My emotions had now become so volatile and so extreme, my nervous responses so near the surface, so rapid and keen, that I was living in another dimension, my heart seemed to beat faster, my step to be quicker, everything I saw was brighter, its outlines more sharply, precisely defined. And all this since yesterday. I had wondered whether I looked different in some essential way so that, when I eventually returned home, my friends and family would notice the change ...

Now answer the following question:

  ✿ **How do the narrator's thoughts and feelings change during this extract?**

Write a full answer, between half a side and a whole side of A4, in about 15 minutes.

Answer this final question of the unit without any support. Track the thoughts and feelings of the narrator systematically. Note that, as the passage advances, the thoughts and feelings of the narrator change.

1 Prose reading

How does the writer convey the thoughts and feelings that you experience in these lines?

How does the writer convey the horror of this event?

How effective are these lines as an ending to the story?

Think about:
- what happens in these lines and how they relate to what has gone before
- the writer's technique and use of language
- why the story is called   .

How does the writer create excitement and suspense in these lines?

Think about:
- what happens in these lines
- the relationships between the characters
- the writer's technique and use of language.

Questions that require a close reading and some understanding of the skills of established writers are often asked in the form 'How does the writer ...?' Such questions can confuse many students because they think that answers have to be written in an expert language that they themselves do not possess. Well, technical language can be handy in support of a sensible comment or two, but you will be relieved to know that it is not make-or-break whether you know the name of a particular technique or whether you can spot an example of it in the text you are studying.

Every writer starts with a blank piece of paper or a blank screen. When the job is done and the text is complete, each word of a polished piece of writing contributes to the effect that the writer is creating. As a student, you must read closely and appreciate the effect of **words**, **phrases**, **images**, **sentences** and **paragraphs** and their contribution to the **whole text**.

Frankly, learning to use technical terms is a long-term business and memorizing them just to patch up your reading skills is not a good idea. In any case, each text is unique – look for a cliffhanger and you might not find one; spot some alliteration and it might not mean anything; find an image and it might not be either a simile or a metaphor! Instead, enjoy and appreciate each text you read and do not be afraid to puzzle out the meaning and how the writer uniquely created it.

Read the following passage from *Tickets, Please* by D.H. Lawrence. It is the opening of the story, setting the scene, on the tram and at the terminus.

During the First World War, with many men in the armed forces fighting abroad, all the conductors on the trams were women. Only the drivers and inspectors were men. The following short passage describes a typical tram journey along a route through a Midlands mining community.

There is in the Midlands a single-line tramway system which boldly leaves the county town and plunges off into the black industrial countryside, up hill and down dale, through the long ugly villages of workmen's houses, over canals and railways, past churches perched high and nobly over the smoke and shadows, through stark, grimy cold little market places, tilting away in a rush past cinemas and shops down to the hollow where the collieries are, then up again, past a little rural church, under the ash trees, on in a rush to the terminus, the last little ugly place of industry, the cold little town that shivers on the edge of the wild, gloomy country beyond. There the green and creamy coloured tram-cars seem to pause and purr with curious satisfaction. But in a few minutes – the clock on the turret of the Co-operative Wholesale Society's shops gives the time – away it starts once more on the adventure. Again there are the reckless swoops downhill, bouncing the loops: again the chilly wait in the hill-top market-place: again the breathless slithering round the precipitous drop under the church: again the patient halts at the loops, waiting for the out-coming car: so on and on, for two long hours, till at last the city looms beyond the fat gas-works, the narrow factories draw near, we are in the sordid streets of the great town, once more we sidle to a stand still at our terminus, abashed by the great crimson and cream-coloured city cars, but still perky, jaunty, somewhat dare-devil, green as a jaunty sprig of parsley out of a black colliery garden.

Now answer the following question:

◆ **How does the writer successfully create the effect of being on a tram journey?**

Here are a few things for you to think about:
a What is described and what happens in these lines;
b The mood and atmosphere;
c The writer's choice of words and phrases.

The story opens with a commentary of the tram-journey. The description is rich in detail, but it is not a static scene, it is one of movement and action. Curiously, people are absent, but the tram itself is full of life.

a What is described and what happens in these lines
Cover the ground quickly – how (where) the description starts; the broad essentials (uphill/downhill; stop/start; through villages, towns and industrial countryside) of the journey; how (where) the journey ends.

b   The mood and atmosphere
Points about the effects created by the sentences – excitement, sense of danger, thrills (and spills?), the rollercoaster effect; how this is created – very long sentences (flowing, breathless or both?), the twists and turns, the slow climbs and the racing sensations; the abrupt halts and the lurching starts; the sense of relief at slowing to a halt.

c   The writer's choice of words and phrases
Annotate (as below) – a host of nouns (locations, landmarks), adjectives (describing the fairly barren, rugged landscape and communities), verbs (showing the extremes of the tram's actions and movements) and adverbs (occasionally aiding the personification of the tram). For example, the verb 'plunges' helps to suggest the effect of sudden, out of control movement.

*There is in the Midlands a single-line tramway system which **boldly** leaves the county town and **plunges** off into the **black industrial countryside**, up hill and down dale, through the **long ugly villages** of workmen's houses, over canals and railways, past churches **perched high and nobly** over the smoke and shadows, through **stark, grimy cold little market places, tilting away in a rush** past cinemas and shops down to the hollow where the collieries are, then up again, past a little rural church, under the ash trees, on in a rush to the terminus, the last little ugly place of industry, the **cold little town that shivers** on the edge of the **wild, gloomy country** beyond.*
(ONE SENTENCE – changing pace, dictated by the commas)

*There the green and creamy coloured tram-cars seem to pause **and purr with curious satisfaction**. But in a few minutes – the clock on the turret of the Co-operative Wholesale Society's shops gives the time – away it starts once more on **the adventure**.*
(PAUSING – catching breath)

*Again there are the **reckless swoops downhill, bouncing the loops**: again the **chilly** wait in the hill-top market-place: again **the breathless slithering** round **the precipitous drop** under the church: again the patient halts at the loops, waiting for the out-coming car: so on and on, for two long hours, till at last **the city looms beyond the fat gas-works**, the narrow factories draw near, we are in **the sordid streets** of the great town, once more we sidle to a stand still at our terminus, **abashed by the great crimson and cream-coloured city cars**, but still **perky, jaunty, somewhat dare-devil**, green as a jaunty sprig of parsley out of a black colliery garden.*
(ONE SENTENCE – colons now as well as commas, suggesting more definite pauses; lurching and twisting)

The overall effect of the vocabulary and the sentence structures is one of the tram taking on a life of its own, and the whole world moving and out of control! It's a memorable piece of descriptive writing.

All the school and several local visitors were assembled in the field. Grimes stood by himself, looking depressed. Mr Prendergast, flushed and unusually vivacious, was talking to the Vicar. As the headmaster's party came into sight the Llanabba Silver Band struck up Men of Harlech.

'Shockin' noise,' commented Lady Circumference graciously.

The head prefect came forward and presented her with a programme, be-ribboned and embossed in gold. Another prefect set a chair for her, she sat down with the Doctor next to her and Lord Circumference on the other side of him.

'Pennyfeather,' cried the Doctor above the band, 'start them racing.'

Philbrick gave Paul a megaphone. 'I found this in the pavilion,' he said. 'I thought it might be useful.'

'Who's that extraordinary man?' asked Lady Circumference.

'He is the boxing coach and swimming professional,' said the doctor. 'A finely developed figure, don't you think?'

'First race,' said Paul through the megaphone, 'under sixteen. Quarter-mile!' He read out Grimes's list of starters.

'What's Tangent doin' in this race?' said Lady Circumference. 'The boy can't run an inch.'

The silver band stopped playing.

'The course,' said Paul, 'starts from the pavilion, goes round the clump of elms …'

'Beeches,' corrected Lady Circumference loudly.

'… and ends in front of the bandstand. Starter, Mr Prendergast; timekeeper, Captain Grimes.'

'I shall say, "Are you ready? One, two, three!" and then fire,' said Mr Prendergast. 'Are you ready? One' – there was a terrific report. 'Oh dear! I'm sorry' – but the race had begun. Clearly Tangent was not going to win; he was sitting on the grass crying because he had been wounded by Mr Prendergast's bullet. Philbrick carried him, wailing dismally, into the refreshment tent, where Dingy helped him off with his shoe. His heel was slightly grazed. Dingy gave him a large slice of cake, and he hobbled out surrounded by a sympathetic crowd.

'That won't hurt him,' said Lady Circumference, 'but I think someone ought to remove the pistol from that old man before he does anything serious.'

'I knew that was going to happen,' said Lord Circumference.

'A most unfortunate beginning,' said the Doctor.

'Am I going to die?' said Tangent, his mouth full of cake.

'For God's sake, look after Prendy,' said Grimes in Paul's ear. 'The man's as tight as a lord, and on one whiskey, too.'

'First blood to me!' said Mr Prendergast gleefully.

'The last race will be run again,' said Paul down the megaphone. 'Starter, Mr Philbrick; timekeeper, Mr Prendergast.'

'On your marks! Get set.' Bang went the pistol, this time without disaster.

Now answer the following question:

◆ **How does the writer make this passage humorous and amusing?**

This is an extract that is full of **visual comedy** – in other words, you have to picture the events in your mind to appreciate them fully. There is also quite a lot of **verbal comedy**, that is, humour based on language.

Use a grid like the one below. Broad areas of humour are identified, but the details need to be worked out and used.

AREAS OF HUMOUR	COMMENT/EXPLANATION
Mathematical names – Circumference etc.	*Silly, but quite funny. Prevents the reader from taking them too seriously ...*
The words and behaviour and attitude of Lady Circumference. Several examples.	*Rude in an upper-class sort of way, even to her own family. Larger-than-life character.*
The shooting – and the reactions to it.	
Prendergast – drunk.	
Tangent – stuffing himself with cake.	

REMEMBER Humour is a personal thing, but any fair reader will admit to the success of this passage in its efforts to show these characters as ridiculous.

Read the following passage from *Billy Liar* by Keith Waterhouse. Billy Fisher is a young man who daydreams to escape the boredom and frustrations of his life in Stradhoughton. He works in a funeral directors' office, but his ambition is to be a scriptwriter in London.

At breakfast with his mother, father and grandmother, Billy raises the topic of his plans to write jokes for the comedian Danny Boon.

I had often likened the conversation at Hillcrest to the route of the old No. 14 tram. Even when completely new subjects were being discussed, the talk rattled on along the familiar track, stopping to load on festering arguments from the past, and culminating at the terminus of the old man's wrath.

'What job with Danny Boon?'

This line – together with a rhubarb-rhubarb chorus of 'What's he talking about, Danny Boon' – was optional for the whole family, but was in fact spoken by my mother.

'The job I was telling you about.'

'What job, you've never told me about no job.'

It was obviously going to be one of the uphill treks. The whole family knew well enough about my ambition, or one of my ambitions, to write scripts for comedy. They knew how Danny Boon, who was not so famous then as he is now, had played a week at the Stradhoughton Empire. They knew, because I had told them four times, that I had taken him some material – including my 'thick as lead' catchline which Boon now uses all the time – and how he had liked it. ('Well how do you know he'll pay you anything?' my mother had said.) They knew I had asked him for a job. Thank God, I thought, as I pushed my boiled egg aside with the yolk gone and the white untouched, that they don't ask me who Danny Boon is when he's at home.

'Why does he always leave the white of his egg?' asked Gran. 'It's all goodness, just thrown down the sink.'

The remark was so completely irrelevant that even my mother, always a willing explorer down the back-doubles on the conversational map, ignored it. Shouts of 'What about your job at Shadrack and Duxbury's?' and 'Who do you think's going to keep you?' began to trickle through but I maintained my hysterical calm, wearing my sensitivity like armour. Above everything I could hear the querulous tones of Gran, going over and over again: 'What's he on about? What's he on about? What's he on about? What's he on about?'

I took a deep breath and made it obvious that I was taking a deep breath, and said: 'Look, there is a comedian. The comedian's name is Danny Boom. B–double O–N. He does not write his own scripts. He gets other people to do it for him. He likes my material. He thinks he can give me regular work.'

My mother said: 'How do you mean, he likes your material?'

I brought out the heavy sigh and the clenched teeth. 'Look. This pepper-pot is Danny Boon. This salt-cellar is my material. Danny Boon is looking for material – ' I turned the blue plastic pepper-pot on them like a ray-gun. 'He sees my flaming material. So he flaming well asks for it.'

''Ere, rear, rear, watch your bloody language! With your flaming this and flaming that! At meal-times! You're not in bloody London yet, you know!'

Now answer the following question:

♣ **How does the writer convey a sense of frustration in Billy Fisher as he tells his story?**

Here are a few things for you to think about:
– what happens in these lines
– how Billy thinks and feels
– how his father, mother and grandmother behave
– the writer's technique and use of language.

Billy is the first-person narrator of this story. Billy's character is presented by Keith Waterhouse through the way he (Billy) tells the story, the way he behaves and the way the people around him behave. Use a grid like the one below to tackle the listed points and build a sustained answer.

What happens in these lines:	Textual references and comments:
How Billy thinks and feels:	Textual references and comments:
How Billy's father, mother and grandmother behave:	Textual references and comments:
The writer's technique and use of language:	Textual references and comments:

Read the following passage from a short story *The Voyage* by Katherine Mansfield. The mother of the little girl, Fenella, has died and Fenella is going away to stay indefinitely with her grandparents. The boat that will take Fenella and her grandmother away is about to leave and her father is saying goodbye.

He sounded stern, but Fenella, eagerly watching him, saw that he looked tired and sad. Mia-oo-oo-O-O! The second whistle blared just above their heads, and a voice like a cry shouted, 'Any more for the gangway?'

'You'll give my love to father,' Fenella saw her father's lips say. And her grandma, very agitated, answered, 'Of course I will, dear. Go now. You'll be left. Go now, Frank. Go now.'

'It's all right, mother. I've got another three minutes.' To her surprise Fenella saw her father take off his hat. He clasped grandma in his arms and pressed her to him. 'God bless you, mother!' she heard him say.

And grandma put her hand, with the black thread glove that was worn through on her ring finger, against his cheek, and she sobbed, 'God bless you, my own brave son!'

This was so awful that Fenella quickly turned her back on them, swallowed once, twice, and frowned terribly at a little green star on a mast head. But she had to turn round again; her father was going.

'Good-bye, Fenella. Be a good girl.' His cold, wet moustache brushed her cheek. But Fenella caught hold of the lapels of his coat.

'How long am I going to stay?' she whispered anxiously. He wouldn't look at her. He shook her off gently, and gently said, 'We'll see about that. Here! Where's your hand?' He pressed something into her palm. 'Here's a shilling in case you should need it.'

A shilling! She must be going away for ever! 'Father!' cried Fenella. But he was gone. He was the last off the ship. The sailors put their shoulders to the gangway. A huge coil of dark rope went flying through the air and fell 'thump' on the wharf. A bell rang; a whistle shrilled. Silently the dark wharf began to slip, to slide, to edge away from them.

Now answer the following question:

♠ **How effectively does the writer create the sadness of the parting?**

Answer this final question of the unit under timed conditions, as you would in an exam. Write at least half an A4 page in about 15 minutes.

This is a fairly broad invitation to write about an emotional scene: three generations of a family saying goodbye at the start of a journey. Work systematically through the details of the passage, pick out some or all of the following 'ingredients' and use them:

– a dramatic situation
– close observation of characters
– choice of words and phrases
– effectiveness of dialogue
– inner thoughts
– external descriptive detail.

Exam tips

♦ When you answer a question on the writer's technique (***How** does the writer ...?*), do not forget the content and the meaning of the text. (**What** the writer says is just as important as **how** s/he says it.)

♦ Do not drop technical language into your answer just to show off. Spotting a simile or alliteration in isolation is useless.

♦ Think of the writer as starting with a blank sheet of paper and respond appreciatively to the skills on display. Read closely and respond honestly to the writer's best efforts.

♦ Make sure your quotations are regular, but short. Quote a word, a phrase and occasionally a sentence, but comment thoughtfully on your quotations rather than leaving them to speak for themselves.

1 Prose reading

Unit 1.4 Empathy

> Imagine you are   . You write an entry in your diary. You include your thoughts and feelings before, during and after these events.
>
> Imagine you are   . Afterwards you tell your friend what has happened and what you feel about the day. Write down what you say.
>
> (Remember that this is a test of understanding and your answer must be closely linked to the text.)

Empathy tasks like the ones above require you to pretend you are a character in a text that you have read. You have to reflect on the situation, as seen by that character, and respond in a way that is believable. Your aim is to show that you understand the situation by recalling accurately whatever has happened. You should also try to capture the personality and attitude of the character as convincingly as possible. Try to do more than outline a series of facts from the passage. Breathe life into your writing on behalf of your character.

You must focus on the words of the text and try to manipulate them into the thoughts and feelings of the character. Empathy tasks here are a test of your **reading** skills. You can expand a little on your character by inventing a small amount of extra detail that is consistent with his or her known behaviour, but do not get carried away with made-up information. Get your ideas firmly from the text.

Read the following passage from *Tickets, Please* by D.H. Lawrence. Look at the complex reactions of Annie to the way John Thomas behaves.

During the First World War, with many men in the armed forces fighting abroad, all the conductors on the trams were women. Only the drivers and inspectors were men. John Thomas, a young inspector, has taken out several of the women and dropped them quickly. Annie had high hopes of John Thomas, but he dropped her too. On Annie's instruction, the women turn against John Thomas and attack him physically at the depot one night.

He only looked at her with hostile eyes.

'Speak!' she said, putting her face devilishly near his.

'What?' he said, almost overcome.

'You've got to choose!' she cried, as if it were some terrible menace, and as if it hurt her that she could not exact more.

'What?' he said, in fear.

'Choose your girl, Coddy. You've got to choose her now. And you'll get your neck broken if you play any more of your tricks, my boy. You're settled now.'

There was a pause. Again he averted his face. He was cunning in his overthrow. He did not give in to them really – no, not if they tore him to bits.

'All right, then,' he said, 'I choose Annie.' His voice was strange and full of malice. Annie let go of him as if he had been a hot coal.

'He's chosen Annie!' said the girls in chorus.

'Me!' cried Annie. She was still kneeling, but away from him. He was still lying prostrate, with averted face. The girls grouped uneasily around.

'Me!' repeated Annie, with a terrible bitter accent.

Then she got up, drawing away from him with strange disgust and bitterness.

'I wouldn't touch him,' she said.

But her face quivered with a kind of agony, she seemed as if she would fall. The other girls turned aside. He remained lying on the floor, with his torn clothes and bleeding, averted face.

'Oh, if he's chosen –' said Polly.

'I don't want him – he can choose again,' said Annie, with the same rather bitter hopelessness.

'Get up,' said Polly, lifting his shoulder. 'Get up.'

He rose slowly, a strange, ragged, dazed creature. The girls eyed him from a distance, curiously, furtively, dangerously.

'Who wants him?' cried Laura, roughly.

'Nobody,' they answered, with contempt. Yet each one of them waited for him to look at her, hoped he would look at her. All except Annie, and something was broken in her.

He, however, kept his face closed and averted from them all. There was a silence of the end. He picked up the torn pieces of his tunic, without knowing what to do with them. The girls stood about uneasily, flushed, panting, tidying their hair and their dress unconsciously, and watching him. He looked at none of them. He espied his cap in a corner, and went and picked it up. He put it on his head, and one of the girls burst into a shrill, hysteric laugh at the sight he presented. He, however, took no heed, but went straight to where his overcoat hung on a peg. The girls moved away from contact with him as if he had been an electric wire. He put on his coat and buttoned it down. Then he rolled his tunic-rags into a bundle, and stood before the locked door, dumbly.

'Open the door, somebody,' said Laura.

'Annie's got the key,' said one.

Annie silently offered the key to the girls. Nora unlocked the door.

'Tit for tat, old man,' she said. 'Show yourself a man, and don't bear a grudge.'

But without a word or a sign he had opened the door and gone, his faced closed, his head dropped.

'That'll learn him,' said Laura.

'Coddy!' said Nora.

'Shut up, for God's sake!' cried Annie fiercely, as if in torture.

Now answer the following question (write at least half a side of A4 paper):

  ✤ **Imagine you are Annie. Write down your thoughts and feelings about what has happened on this particular night.**

This is a powerful passage and it is a challenge to get inside Annie's head. If you can represent the mixture of love and hate, triumph and regret, your response will be very successful. Adrenaline is high because the girls have just physically attacked John Thomas in revenge for his widespread flirting and two-timing. And remember that, in the midst of all this, the girls who are attacking John Thomas together ... are all rivals of one another for his affection!

Look at the feelings that are associated with Annie through the passage: **devilish, menacing, bitter, disgusted, agonized, hopeless, broken, tortured.**

Look at the reactions of the other girls: **uneasy, curious, furtive, dangerous, contemptuous, flushed.**

Look at John Thomas: **hostile, fearful, cunning** through to the final description of him '... *his face closed, his head dropped.*'

Consider the following:
– the situation at the start of the passage
– the way John Thomas behaves and speaks
– the way the tension holds as the girls surround him
– the way the situation calms down in anti-climax
– the changing feelings of Annie throughout; the way she speaks and behaves at different points.

The following grid offers detailed support, particularly for the opening stages. As a further stage in your preparation for a quality empathy response, copy the grid and write more comments by Annie down the right-hand column.

POINTS OF RELEVANCE IN THE PASSAGE	WHAT ANNIE MIGHT SAY DIRECTLY
Coddy's hostile eyes looking at her.	*He stared at me, hating me ...*
'Speak!' 'You've got to choose!' 'Choose your girl, Coddy.'	*I had to make him choose, I had to know which one of us he really wanted.*
Puts her face 'devilishly' near his. 'And you'll get your neck broken if you play any more tricks, my boy.'	*I felt in control, I felt as if there was an evil strength running through me.*
John Thomas chooses Annie; the girls' reaction.	*He chose me and for a moment I felt triumphant because ... but ...*
Annie's reaction: 'I don't want him ...' etc.	
The silence, followed by John Thomas putting himself back together. The girls' reaction at this point.	
The ending. The dejected image of John Thomas. Last words from the girls, then Annie.	

Read the following passage from *The Ragged Trousered Philanthropists* by Robert Tressell.

The book charts a year in the lives of a group of painters and decorators in the town of Mugsborough at the start of the 20th century. Haunted by fear of unemployment, the men struggle to keep their jobs at any cost, though they realize that their condition of miserable poverty is neither 'natural' nor 'just'.

Hunter the manager, known as Misery, pays a snap visit to check up on the men and their work on the renovation of a house. Look closely at the effect Hunter's presence has on the men, especially Jack Linden.

Linden was still working at the vestibule doors when the manager came downstairs. Misery stood watching him for some minutes without speaking. At last he said loudly:

'How much longer are you going to be messing about those doors? Why don't you get them under colour? You were fooling about there when I was here this morning. Do you think it'll pay to have you playing about there hour after hour with a bit of pumice-stone? Get the work done! Or if you don't want to, I'll very soon find someone else who does! I've been noticing your style of doing things for some time past and I want you to understand that you can't play the fool with me. There's plenty of better men than you walking about. If you can't do more than you've been doing lately you can clear out; we can do without you even when we're busy.'

Old Jack trembled. He tried to answer, but was unable to speak. If he had been a slave and had failed to satisfy his master, the latter might have tied him up somewhere and thrashed him. Hunter could not do that; he could only take his food away. Old Jack was frightened – it was not only *his* food that might be taken away. At last, with a great effort, for the words seemed to stick in his throat, he said:

'I must clean the work down, sir, before I go on painting.'

'I'm not talking about what you're doing, but the time it takes you to do it!' shouted Hunter. 'And I don't want any back answers or argument about it. You just move yourself a bit quicker or leave it alone altogether.'

Linden did not answer: he went on with his work, his hand trembling to such an extent that he was scarcely able to hold the pumice stone.

Hunter shouted so loud that his voice filled all the house. Everyone heard and was afraid. Who would be the next? they thought.

Finding that Linden made no further answer, Misery again began walking about the house.

As he looked at them the men did their work in a nervous, clumsy, hasty sort of way. They made all sorts of mistakes and messes. Payne, the foreman carpenter, was putting some new boards in a part of the drawing-room floor: he was in such a state of panic that, while driving a nail, he accidentally struck the thumb of his left hand a severe blow with his hammer. Bundy was also working in the drawing-room, putting some white-glazed tiles in the fireplace. Whilst cutting one of these in half in order to fit into its place, he inflicted a deep gash on one of his fingers. He was afraid to leave off to bind it up while Hunter was there, and consequently as he worked the white tiles became all smeared and splattered with blood. Easton, who was working with Harlow on a plank, washing off the old distemper from the hall ceiling, was so upset that he was scarcely able to stand on the plank, and presently the brush fell from his trembling hand with a crash upon the floor.

Everyone was afraid. They knew that it was almost impossible to get a job from any other firm. They knew that this man had the power to deprive them of the means of earning a living; that he possessed the power to deprive their children of bread.

Now answer the following question:
- **Imagine you are Jack Linden. At home, you tell your wife about the events of the day at work.**

This should be a fairly straightforward situation to work out and respond to. Hunter (Misery) the manager comes along out of the blue to shake up the men. He is a bully and proceeds to pressurize and threaten Jack Linden and the others, almost one by one. Of course, the more he stands over them, the more nervous they become.

As regards Jack Linden's individual character and situation, which you should try to represent in your response, we know that he is old and particularly nervous, probably a little slower than the others and therefore more likely to be laid off.

You might begin by saying:

'I could feel Misery standing there for minutes on end, but I decided to ignore him and just carried on smoothing down the surface before I started painting. The trouble is he doesn't want a proper job doing, he just wants it all finished double quick speed ...'

Either copy this opening and continue the account or re-start in your own way.

The important things to consider and cover in the account are:
- what Misery says and how he speaks and behaves
- Jack Linden's fears for his own situation
- what happened to Payne, Bundy and Easton
- Jack Linden's thoughts and feelings on what he has seen and experienced
- any wider views Jack may have on the world of employment.

Read the following passage from the comic novel *Cold Comfort Farm* by Stella Gibbons.

Flora Poste has been expensively educated and brought up by friends, while her parents travelled widely. When she is orphaned at the age of 20, she goes looking for relatives and makes contact by letter with the doomed Starkadders of the remote Cold Comfort Farm.

Flora arrives at Cold Comfort Farm at night, having been picked up from the station by Adam Starkadder in his cart, drawn by Viper, a vicious gelding.

'Are we nearly there?'

'Aye, Robert Poste's child.'

And in another five minutes Viper stopped, of his own will, at a gate which Flora could just see in the obscurity. Adam struck him with the whip. He did not move.

'I think we must be there,' observed Flora.

'Nay, niver say that.'

'But I do say it. Look – if you drive on we shall go slam into a hedge.'

' 'Tes all one, Robert Poste's child.'

'It may be all right for you, and all one, but it isn't to me. I shall get down.'

So she did; and found her way slowly, through darkness only lit by faint winter starlight, along a villainous muddy path between hedges, which was too narrow for the buggy to enter.

Adam followed her, carrying the lantern, and leaving Viper at the gate.

The buildings of the farm, a shade darker than the sky, could now be distinguished in the gloom, a little distance on, and as Flora and Adam were slowly approaching them a door suddenly opened and a beam of light shone out. Adam gave a joyful cry.

''Tes the cowshed! 'Tes our Feckless openin' the door for me!' And Flora saw that it was indeed; the door of the shed, which was lit by a lantern, was being anxiously pushed open by the nose of a gaunt cow.

This was not promising.

But immediately a deep voice was heard: 'Is that you, Adam?' and a woman came out of the cowshed, carrying the lantern, which she lifted high above her head to look at the travellers. Flora dimly discerned an unnecessarily red and voluminous shawl on her shoulders, and a tumbling mass of hair.

'Oh, how do you do?' she called. 'You must be my Cousin Judith. I'm so glad to see you. How nice of you to come out in all this cold. Terribly nice of you to have me, too. Isn't it curious we should never have met before?'

She put out her hand, but it was not taken at once. The lantern was lifted higher while Judith steadily looked into her face, in silence. The seconds passed. Flora wondered if her lipstick were the wrong shade. It then occurred to her that there was a less frivolous cause for the silence which had fallen and for the steady regard with which her cousin confronted her. So, Flora mused, must Columbus have felt when the poor Indian fixed his solemn, unwavering gaze upon the great sailor's face. For the first time a Starkadder looked upon a civilized being.

But one could weary even of this; and Flora soon did. She asked Judith if Judith would think her terribly rude if she did not meet the rest of the family that evening. Might she, Flora, just have a morsel of food in her own room?

1 Prose reading

'It is cold there,' said Judith, draggingly, at last.

'Oh, a fire will soon warm it up,' said Flora, firmly. 'Too nice of you, I do think, to take so much care of me.'

'My sons, Seth and Reuben –' Judith choked on the words, then recovered, and added in a lower voice, 'My sons are waiting to see their cousin.'

This seemed to Flora, in conjunction with their ominous names, too like a cattle show, so she smiled vaguely and said it was so nice of them, but she thought, all the same, she would see them in the morning.

Now answer this question:

* **Imagine you are Flora Poste. You write immediately after these events to tell your best friend in London about your initial experience at Cold Comfort Farm.**

Here are a few thoughts to help you:

Flora is bright and independent so she should be able to cope with the primitive life of the Starkadders. In writing to her friend in London, she will certainly have something to say about Adam and Viper, Feckless and the cowshed. Then there is Judith, whose appearance would be worthy of much comment, and the silence, that is explained quite grandly in the text. Flora is confident enough, and probably cheeky, to ask for food in her room. She's pleasant and polite, but she's feeling the contrast between her sophistication and the Starkadders' primitive ways and cannot handle too much of them at once.

A really good response to this question will capture some of Flora's friendly snootiness as well as her observations about the Starkadders.

Read the following passage from *Extraordinary Little Cough* by Dylan Thomas. It is taken from a collection of his short stories called *Portrait of the Artist as a Young Dog*. These stories celebrate the vitality of youth and the eccentricity of common life. The narrator of this story (Dylan) is one of a group of four boys out camping in their summer holidays. The group is invaded by two school bullies, Brazell and Scully, and then joined also by three girls.

In this passage, George Hooping (Little Cough to his friends) is out of his depth with the girls and goes off instead to prove to Brazell and Skully that he can run across Rhossili Sands. The rest of the boys and the girls spend their time flirting.

I spoke to Jean alone; and this is love, I thought, as she nodded her head and swung her curls and said: 'It's nicer than Porthcawl.'

Brazell and Skully were two big bullies in a nightmare; I forgot them when Jean and I walked up the cliff, and, looking back to see if they were baiting George again or wrestling together, I saw that George had disappeared around the corner of the rocks and that they were talking at the foot of the cliff with Sidney and the two girls.

'What's your name?'

I told her.

'That's Welsh,' she said.

'You've got a beautiful name.'

'Oh, it's just ordinary.'

'Shall I see you again?'

'If you want to.'

'I want to all right! We can go and bathe in the morning. And we can try to get an eagle's egg. Did you know that there were eagles here?'

'No,' she said. 'Who was that handsome boy on the beach, the tall one with dirty trousers?'

'He's not handsome, that's Brazell. He never washes or combs his hair or anything. He's a bully and he cheats.'

'I think he's handsome.'

We walked into Button's field, and I showed her inside the tents and gave her one of George's apples. 'I'd like a cigarette,' she said.

It was nearly dark when the others came. Brazell and Skully were with Gwyneth, one each side of her holding her arms, Sidney was with Peggy, and Dan walked, whistling, behind with his hands in his pockets.

'There's a pair,' said Brazell, 'they've been here all alone and they aren't even holding hands. You want a pill,' he said to me.

'Build Britain's Babies,' said Skully.

'Go on!' Gwyneth said. She pushed him away from her, but she was laughing, and she said nothing when he put his arms around her waist.

'What about a bit of fire?' said Brazell.

Jean clapped her hands like an actress. Although I knew I loved her, I didn't like anything she said or did.

'Who's going to make it?'

'He's the best, I'm sure,' she said, pointing at me.

Dan and I collected sticks, and by the time it was quite dark there was a fire crackling. Inside the sleeping-tent, Brazell and Jean sat close together; her

1 Prose reading

golden head was on his shoulder;
Skully, near them, whispered to
Gwyneth; Sidney unhappily held
Peggy's hand.

'Did you ever see such a
sloppy lot?' I said, watching Jean
smile in the fiery dark.

'Kiss me, Charley!' said Dan.

We sat by the fire in the
corner of the field. The sea, far out,
was still making a noise. We heard a
few nightbirds. 'Tu-whit! Tu-whoo!
Listen! I don't like owls,' Dan said,
'they scratch your eyes out!' — and
tried not to listen to the soft voices
in the tent. Gwyneth's laughter
floated out over the suddenly
moonlit field, but Jean, with the
beast, was smiling and silent in the
covered warmth; I knew her little
hand was in Brazell's hand.

'Women!' I said.

Dan spat in the fire.

We were old and alone, sitting
beyond desire in the middle of the
night, when George appeared, like a
ghost, in the firelight and stood there
trembling until I said: 'Where've you
been? You've been gone hours. Why
are you trembling like that?'

Brazell and Skully poked their
heads out.

'Hallo, Cough my boy! How's
your father? What have you been up
to to-night?'

George Hooping could hardly
stand. I put my hand on his shoulder
to steady him, but he pushed it away.

'I've been running on Rhossilli
sands! I ran every bit of it! You said I
couldn't, and I did! I've been running
and running!'

Now answer the following question:

♣ **Imagine you are Jean. The day after these events you write an entry in your diary. You include your thoughts and feelings about meeting the boys.**

Answer this question under timed conditions, as you would in an exam. Write at least half a side of A4 paper in about 15 minutes.

You might like to consider the following points:
– She is with the narrator (Dylan) at first, walking and talking.
– She shows an interest in Brazell and goes with him.
– She may comment on what she sees, including George.
– There are details about Jean in the text that may relate to her personality.

Exam tips

♣ Remember that an empathy task in this section is a test of **reading** skills, so concentrate your efforts on writing about details from the text.
♣ Try to think your way into the character's situation. Then you will succeed in sounding like the character and in expressing his or her thoughts and feelings directly.
♣ You do not have to start with the first thing that happened to your character. Start with the main thing that would be on his or her mind.

Descriptive and imaginative writing

GCSE English Paper 1

Section B (Writing:15%) will test **descriptive** and **imaginative** writing through two tasks. The first will ask for a piece of writing to *inform, explain, describe*. The second will offer opportunities for a variety of approaches in writing to *explore, imagine, entertain*.

Good writing defies the labels that people sometimes like to use. For example, an interesting narrative will certainly have descriptive qualities, while a piece of autobiographical writing is bound to have a great deal of imaginative, even fictional, content.

Fortunately, writing to *inform, explain, describe* and *explore, imagine, entertain* encourages, rather than restricts, good writing under examination conditions by recognizing the potential for a range of qualities in a single task. Thus, a task that requires descriptive qualities hopes to draw out pieces of writing that genuinely engage the reader by also informing and explaining.

When your examination writing is marked, it will be assessed in terms of:
a content and organization
b sentence structure, punctuation and spelling.

This section of the book contains three units:

2.1 Writing to *inform, explain, describe* You will learn about the content and organization of descriptive writing.

2.2 Writing to *explore, imagine, entertain* You will learn about the content and organization of imaginative writing.

2.3 Technical accuracy in descriptive and imaginative writing You will examine sentence structure, punctuation and spelling in relation to descriptive and imaginative writing.

Unit 2.1 Writing to inform, explain, describe

A sense of place

Describing a scene in detail and bringing it to life is known as creating a 'sense of place'. Remember that any *description* that you write will also be *informing* the reader and *explaining* the scene or the events described. A good description will mean that readers can imagine that they are actually in the place described, even if they have no experience of it themselves.

♣ The key to creating a good sense of place is to imagine yourself in the scene you are describing. Focus on all of your senses so that your writing has depth.

♣ You should not write a story about the scene you are describing. You should just focus on describing the scene itself in as much detail as possible.

Below are some examples of the sorts of task that you could be given in the exam.

Write a description of a market at a busy time.

Describe the scene on a beach or in a park on a summer's day.

Describe the scene in a large shopping centre on Christmas Eve.

Describe the scene in a dining hall or canteen at lunchtime.

In this unit, you will be taken through a series of steps designed to improve the effectiveness of your writing. In an exam, however, you will only have time to plan in your head and then check quickly at the end. You will not have the time to draft and re-draft your response.

Group work

In pairs or a small group, make a list of places that you could describe effectively from memory or from your imagination. These could be general, such as a beach or a market, or specific, such as a particular zoo or airport. You could make a sub-list of beauty spots and a further sub-list of places that are environmental disasters or eyesores.

Think of places that you can visualize clearly and can recollect in detail. Discuss which ones are personal to you, which ones would be favoured by particular types of student and which ones could appear in an exam as a fair challenge to everyone.

---

2 Descriptive and imaginative writing

When you start to write about a scene, you should focus on what you imagine you would actually **see** if you were there.

Read the following description of a market at a busy time.

The market is full of brightly coloured stalls selling everything you could possibly imagine: exotic fruits, fish, hand-made ornaments, spices, fabrics. There are people everywhere, pushing and shoving. They do not care about anyone else; they just focus on grabbing the bargains first. The shoppers are carrying enormous bulging carrier bags, already full to the brim with purchases. There is no room to walk in-between the market stalls because the area is so full of people and I have to barge my way through just like everyone else.

In the above description, the writer focuses primarily on the sights that can be seen at the market. There are many other sights that could be included, such as two shoppers arguing over an item on a stall, and the writer could expand on exactly what is being sold at each stand.

Now complete the following task:
* **Write a description of a funfair.**
For the purposes of this exercise, focus primarily on what you can see, rather than any of the other senses.

The following description of a market includes descriptions of the sounds as well as things that can be seen. This adds a bit more depth to the writing. When the writer develops the scene like this, the reader will begin to get a sense of place.

The market is full of brightly coloured stalls selling everything you could possibly imagine: exotic fruits, fish, hand-made ornaments, spices, fabrics. *The market sellers shout at the tops of their voices to attract the attention of the shoppers.* There are people everywhere, pushing and shoving. *They yell at each other to move out of the way and complain and mutter under their breath about each other.* They do not care about anyone else; they just focus on grabbing the bargains first. The shoppers are carrying enormous bulging carrier bags, already full to the brim with purchases. There is no room to walk in-between the market stalls because the area is so full of people and I have to barge my way through, *shouting at them to move out of my way just like everyone else. Over all of the noise, I hear a stallholder shouting 'candyfloss' and I make my way towards him.*

Now complete the following task:

◆ **Describe the scene in a park on a summer's day.**

Remember to use a range of senses but do not force each sense into your writing in equal amounts. Write naturally.

People

People feature in most scenes. In a busy scene, the people may appear as a crowd, without any sense of individuality, either in appearance or in personality.

Generalizing about the people in a scene is understandable:
The families scramble over the sunbathers ... The children throw off their shorts and T-shirts ...
but why not add observations of the appearance and behaviour of single characters?
The smallest child struggles behind the rest and falls headlong in the sand, his dignity lost.

Names

Without names, you can still create a sense of place, but perhaps not the sense of a **particular** place. Contrast a crowd of 70,000 people singing 'Land of my Fathers' in the Millennium Stadium, Cardiff with the Belle Vue ground at Rhyl where 200 or so loyal supporters, including a coachload supporting the visitors, huddle under umbrellas to escape the horizontal rain.

What about the man on the beach reading the paper? Is it the *Sun* or the *Daily Telegraph*?

The familiar woman serving chips in the canteen – is she Pat or Lil?

Names of people, places and items can add a great deal to the realism and originality of your writing.

Dialogue

Brief snatches of dialogue can work well in descriptive writing.

Sometimes, only one contribution is needed, e.g. a newspaper seller shouting *'Late Final Echooooo ... !'*

Elsewhere, a quick exchange can work:
'Mam, can I have an ice-cream?'
'I've told you no, now shut up!'

However, too much dialogue could spoil the effect.

Nouns and verbs

It is not just adjectives and adverbs that contribute to descriptive language – nouns and verbs do too.

Striding, ambling, dawdling – each describes a particular way of 'walking'.
Bungalow, cottage, villa – all offer a more precise image than 'house'.

2 Descriptive and imaginative writing

Now complete the following task:

◆ **Add the *smells* and *tastes* you experience at the funfair to your description.**

The final sense is **touch**. It is easy to insert touch into your description *but do not forget to express your emotions too*. These describe how and what you feel and will add the most depth to your writing. You should also include your opinions on what is being experienced. For example, do you like the busy market place? Do you enjoy shopping in the January sales? Do you feel exhilarated or do you feel threatened and uncomfortable?

Read the following description of a beach on a summer's day.

The sun is beating down on the beach. The seagulls caw overhead and then dive into the depths of the sea. Rows and rows of brightly coloured cars are parked like regimental soldiers. Families emerge from them and the children run eagerly towards the sea. The parents run clumsily after them, arms full of picnic food, deckchairs, windbreakers and every conceivable item needed for a day at the beach. Anxious mums and dads call to their excited children to be careful over the wet rocks, but their calls cannot be heard above the excited chatter coming up from the beach. The salty air smacks you in the face as you reach the large grey rocks that mark the start of the beach. Mingled with the salt is the smell of barbecued food that makes your mouth water with anticipation.

    The families scramble over the sunbathers and try to find an empty square foot of the golden beach to lay out their towels and unpack their picnics. The children throw off their shorts and T-shirts and hurry to the water. The wet sand squelches between their toes and makes them squeal with delight. From their place on the beach, the parents can only just pick out the multi-coloured dot in the distance that is their child.

Now complete the following task:

♣ **Describe the scene in a park on a summer's day.**

Remember to use a range of senses but do not force each sense into your writing in equal amounts. Write naturally.

People

People feature in most scenes. In a busy scene, the people may appear as a crowd, without any sense of individuality, either in appearance or in personality.

Generalizing about the people in a scene is understandable:

The families scramble over the sunbathers ... The children throw off their shorts and T-shirts ...

but why not add observations of the appearance and behaviour of single characters?

The smallest child struggles behind the rest and falls headlong in the sand, his dignity lost.

Names

Without names, you can still create a sense of place, but perhaps not the sense of a **particular** place. Contrast a crowd of 70,000 people singing 'Land of my Fathers' in the Millennium Stadium, Cardiff with the Belle Vue ground at Rhyl where 200 or so loyal supporters, including a coachload supporting the visitors, huddle under umbrellas to escape the horizontal rain.

What about the man on the beach reading the paper? Is it the *Sun* or the *Daily Telegraph*?

The familiar woman serving chips in the canteen – is she Pat or Lil?

Names of people, places and items can add a great deal to the realism and originality of your writing.

Dialogue

Brief snatches of dialogue can work well in descriptive writing.

Sometimes, only one contribution is needed, e.g. a newspaper seller shouting *'Late Final Echooooo ... !'*

Elsewhere, a quick exchange can work:
'Mam, can I have an ice-cream?'
'I've told you no, now shut up!'

However, too much dialogue could spoil the effect.

Nouns and verbs

It is not just adjectives and adverbs that contribute to descriptive language – nouns and verbs do too.

Striding, ambling, dawdling – each describes a particular way of 'walking'.
Bungalow, cottage, villa – all offer a more precise image than 'house'.

2 Descriptive and imaginative writing

When you start to write about a scene, you should focus on what you imagine you would actually **see** if you were there.

Read the following description of a market at a busy time.

The market is full of brightly coloured stalls selling everything you could possibly imagine: exotic fruits, fish, hand-made ornaments, spices, fabrics. There are people everywhere, pushing and shoving. They do not care about anyone else; they just focus on grabbing the bargains first. The shoppers are carrying enormous bulging carrier bags, already full to the brim with purchases. There is no room to walk in-between the market stalls because the area is so full of people and I have to barge my way through just like everyone else.

In the above description, the writer focuses primarily on the sights that can be seen at the market. There are many other sights that could be included, such as two shoppers arguing over an item on a stall, and the writer could expand on exactly what is being sold at each stand.

Now complete the following task:
- ♣ **Write a description of a funfair.**
For the purposes of this exercise, focus primarily on what you can see, rather than any of the other senses.

The following description of a market includes descriptions of the sounds as well as things that can be seen. This adds a bit more depth to the writing. When the writer develops the scene like this, the reader will begin to get a sense of place.

The market is full of brightly coloured stalls selling everything you could possibly imagine: exotic fruits, fish, hand-made ornaments, spices, fabrics. *The market sellers shout at the tops of their voices to attract the attention of the shoppers.* There are people everywhere, pushing and shoving. *They yell at each other to move out of the way and complain and mutter under their breath about each other.* They do not care about anyone else; they just focus on grabbing the bargains first. The shoppers are carrying enormous bulging carrier bags, already full to the brim with purchases. There is no room to walk in-between the market stalls because the area is so full of people and I have to barge my way through, *shouting at them to move out of my way just like everyone else. Over all of the noise, I hear a stallholder shouting 'candyfloss' and I make my way towards him.*

Now complete the following task:

♣ **Read back over your description of the funfair. Expand on your description to include the sounds you can *hear* as well as the sights of the funfair.**

To build up your answer you might like to consider:
- the noise of the people at the fair, laughing, shouting, screaming or cheering
- the noises of the rides at the fair, like the ghost train, the waltzers and the dodgems
- the noises from the stallholders
- any music being played
- any other sounds you can think of.

Your description should now be more realistic, but to enhance it even more you can include the other senses too. The smells experienced in these scenes can add real depth to your writing, as can the things you can taste. The reader can imagine these smells and tastes and this creates a strong sense of place. Using the market example, it is possible to insert these senses into the description.

The market is full of brightly coloured stalls selling everything you could possibly imagine: exotic fruits, fish, hand-made ornaments, spices, fabrics. *My nose is filled with a strange mix of smells. As I walk past the fish stall, the air is filled with salty smells that remind me of the sea and I can almost taste the salt on my tongue.* The market sellers shout at the tops of their voices to attract the attention of the shoppers. There are people everywhere, pushing and shoving. They yell at each other to move out of the way and complain and mutter under their breath about each other. They do not care about anyone else; they just focus on grabbing the bargains first. *I move towards the spice stall and my nose is filled with exotic smells that make it itch and make me want to sneeze.* The shoppers are carrying enormous bulging carrier bags, already full to the brim with purchases. There is no room to walk in-between the market stalls because the area is so full of people and I have to barge my way through, shouting at them to move out of my way just like everyone else. Over all of the noise, I hear a stallholder shouting 'candyfloss' and I make my way towards him. *The stall offers a huge variety of sweets and I can smell the hot sweet aroma of toffee from the toffee apples lined up along the front of the stall. I order a bag of candyfloss and the sweet pink sugar dissolves on my tongue.*

The weather

Weather can easily be forgotten as an important feature of an outdoor scene. The climate in Britain is rarely extreme, but it is nearly always changeable. The changes can be quite subtle – for example, rain can move from *drizzle* to *sleet*, while clouds can be *wispy* or *threatening*.

Well-judged observations about the weather can make descriptive writing more effective.

Movement

To add interest to your description, you could add some sort of movement to it. This can be done in several ways:

1   Describe yourself walking through the scene. This means describing the scene in the first person.
    *As **I** walk through the market **I** can see …*

2   Describe the scene as it would be seen by someone else. This means writing the story in the second person.
    *As **you** walk through the market **you** can see …*

3   Describe the scene in the present tense to make it more 'immediate'.
    *As I **walk** through the market I **can see** someone haggling over the price of a purchase. Then someone **barges** into me and I nearly **fall over** with the force of it.*

Now complete the following tasks:

♣   **Describe the scene in a large shopping centre on Christmas Eve.**
Consider all of the points that have been covered in this unit.

♣   **Return to your group list of possible scenes and locations for a descriptive piece. Choose one of them and write a full answer.**
Write about one side of A4 paper under timed conditions in 25 minutes.

> ### Exam tips
>
> ♣   Do not fall into the trap of saying 'I can't do this well because the title is boring'. A title is not long enough to be boring! Take on the task with some enthusiasm and vision.
>
> ♣   Do not overuse adjectives and adverbs in your writing, e.g. *'The happy young children ran joyfully across the beautiful golden sands to the azure blue sea where the gentle waves playfully awaited them.'* This is known as 'writing by numbers'!
>
> ♣   Write honestly about a scene you can visualize and develop using a range of senses (e.g. hearing, smell, taste and touch). Write in clear, varied sentences. Do not settle for a tired old formula with one well-practised trick or feature. Write freely.
>
> ♣   Make sure your writing is accurate. Be very careful with your basic skills and general presentation. Use Unit 2.3 at the end of this section to help you with your technical accuracy.

Narratives

A narrative is a written (or spoken) account of connected events. It is creative (*exploring* the subject matter), *imaginative*, and designed to *entertain* the reader. A writer creates a narrative using descriptions, action and dialogue, and makes the story seem as believable and convincing as possible.

The key to writing a narrative is to stay focused on the title or theme – do not drift away from the main subject of the story.

Below are some examples of possible titles and personal topics, opening and closing lines for narratives which you might be asked to write about in the exam.

Titles
A time for celebration
A most unlikely hero
Living in the past

Personal topics
Write about a time when you felt very nervous.
Write about a time when you upset your best friend.
Write about an incident which taught you the value of money.

Openings (Continue the following ...)
Suddenly the phone went dead ...
I had never liked mobile phones and now I knew why ...
It was my first day at school and all I knew was that I wanted it to be over as soon as possible ...

Endings (Write a story that ends with these words ...)
... Just at that moment, I heard the car draw up outside and I knew I was in deep, deep trouble.
... But I will never forget the look on her face.
... And I hope you feel proud of yourself.

In this unit you will be taken through a series of steps designed to improve the effectiveness of your writing. In an exam, however, you will only have time to plan in your head and then check quickly at the end. You will not have the time to draft and re-draft your response.

Group work

In pairs or small groups, make lists of possible titles, personal topics, opening lines and closing lines (endings) to expand the choices offered on page 50.

Before you start to write a narrative, think carefully about how your story will progress.

a You could write your story in the first person, drawing from your own experience.

*I love Christmas. It is **my** favourite time of year. But last year, **I** didn't enjoy Christmas at all ...*

b Alternatively, you could write your story based around a character.

*As **Richard** opened his birthday present **his** face dropped. **His** mother had bought **him** a book about a little fluffy rabbit. This was not what **he** had asked for. **His** mother smiled expectantly at **him** and **he** faked a smile in return and said, 'Thanks, mum. It's perfect!'*

When writing your story, describe the actions in detail so that the reader knows exactly what is going on.

Read the following on the personal topic '*A time when I felt nervous*'.

The Christmas concert was the highlight of the school year for teachers, parents and pupils alike. The Deputy Head wrote a new story every year. We had all been through the auditions and rehearsed our lines carefully. Before we knew it the night of the concert had arrived. Parents were filing into the school hall and pushing and shoving each other in an attempt to get the best seats for watching the play.

The room fell silent as the Head Mistress walked out onto the middle of the stage and welcomed everyone to the school. I stood behind the curtain to the left of the stage, waiting for my cue. I held my breath as tiny beads of sweat ran down my forehead. My stomach was fluttering wildly and I had a huge lump in my throat. My heart quickened. My cue was coming nearer. It was nearly my turn to go out onto the stage. In a flash of panic, I realized that I couldn't remember my opening lines. I looked around quickly for Sam who had a copy of the script, but I couldn't see him anywhere.

Then suddenly I heard it – the cue for my entrance. What was I going to do?

In the above story (narrative), the writer primarily focuses on his feelings when he was nervous. This description is very detailed and allows the reader to understand exactly how the writer felt. However, the writer has not included dialogue in his description. Dialogue would make the piece of writing seem even more real.

Now complete the following task:

◆ **Write about a time when you felt very surprised.**

For the purposes of this exercise, focus primarily on the actions rather than the dialogue in your story.

The following response includes dialogue as well as the writer's actions and emotions. This makes the story more real and convincing. However, in the same way that you should not write the whole story just with action, do not be tempted to write the story completely in dialogue. You need a good combination of both to make your story a success.

The Christmas concert was the highlight of the school year for teachers, parents and pupils alike. The Deputy Head wrote a new story every year. We had all been through the auditions and rehearsed our lines carefully. Before we knew it the night of the concert had arrived. Parents were filing into the school hall and pushing and shoving each other in an attempt to get the best seats for watching the play. *They were all whispering about how proud they were about their children, 'My son is a shepherd', 'My daughter is Mary', 'My son is a sheep!'*

The room fell silent as the Head Mistress walked out onto the middle of the stage and welcomed everyone to the school. *'Good evening, ladies and gentlemen and welcome to Holly Primary School's Christmas play.'*

I stood behind the curtain to the left of the stage, waiting for my cue. I held my breath as tiny beads of sweat ran down my forehead. My stomach was fluttering wildly and I had a huge lump in my throat. My heart quickened. My cue was coming nearer. It was nearly my turn to go out onto the stage. In a flash of panic, I realized that I couldn't remember my opening lines. I looked around quickly for Sam who had a copy of the script, but I couldn't see him anywhere. *'Sam! Sam!' I whispered frantically, but all I got in reply was a 'Shhh!' from Mrs Walsh.*

Then suddenly I heard it – the cue for my entrance, *'So here to introduce the concert properly is Josh, our narrator.'* What was I going to do?

Now complete the following task:

◆ **Read back over your story about feeling surprised. Expand on your writing to include dialogue as well as actions.**

If you are given the title for the story, make sure you write just about that topic. Stay focused on the task and make sure your story captures the theme given in the title.

2 Descriptive and imaginative writing

Read the following start to a story with the title 'A time for celebration'.

For nearly nine long months I had waited to meet my new brother or sister. I had watched my mother slowly getting bigger and bigger and I had laid my head on her and felt the baby kicking. I had helped my father paint the spare bedroom and I had helped to decorate it with brand new toys and equipment.

In the middle of the night on a Tuesday, my dad woke me up from a dreamy sleep, whispering, 'It's time! We're going to the hospital.'

I gathered my suitcase and helped him get mum and her suitcase into our car. They took me to gran's house where I was to stay until the baby was born. Every few hours the next day, dad would ring and say, 'No news yet.' Gran tried to amuse me with stories about when mum was having me but all I could think about was my new baby brother or sister.

This story clearly introduces the reason for the **celebration** in its opening lines – the writer's mother is expecting a baby. In this case, the writer is clearly focusing specifically on the given title. In many cases, the connection between the opening and the title is more subtle.

Now complete the following task:
- ♣ **Write the opening paragraph for a story based on the title 'The visit'.**

Some narrative writing tasks may need a personal response. For these tasks you are required to describe an event from your own experience. You must write these tasks in the first person, using 'I', 'me' and 'my'. Remember to include your thoughts and feelings along with dialogue and action when completing these tasks.

Read the following start to a story in response to the personal topic '*Write about a time when you upset your best friend*'.

When we started in secondary school Amy and I were the best of friends. That was until we met Jack. Amy and I liked all the same things, dressed in the same way and even looked the same. People were always getting us confused because we were so similar. Naturally, this similarity meant that we also liked the same people – including boys. Jack was the fastest runner in our year group and was captain of the athletics team. Amy and I had talked very often about how much we both liked him.

'I love his eyes,' I said. 'They're the bluest eyes I've ever seen.'

'I love how fast he can run,' said Amy. 'It's no wonder he's the captain. Everyone thinks he's fantastic.'

'Including us!' I said and we both laughed.

I knew she liked Jack as much as I did, but even our friendship didn't stop me trying to talk to Jack alone.

In this story, the writer describes an event from her own experience. She writes the story in the first person and includes conversation in her writing to make her story more realistic.

Now complete the following task:

+ **Write the opening paragraph of a story in response to: 'Write about a time when you took part in sport.'**

For some narrative writing tasks, you might be given the opening line for a story. Although it sounds obvious, make sure your story opens with the given line. Do not use your own opening line. Also make sure that your story continues the theme or topic presented in the opening line. Make sure your story logically follows on from the line given.

Read the following start to a story in response to: *'Write a story that follows on from "Suddenly the phone went dead ... "'*

Suddenly the phone went dead. Rachel screamed into the phone, 'Why are you doing this to me?' Then her scream turned into a whisper as she began to cry, 'Hello? Hello?'

Rachel had started going to Black Forest High School in the September before, two whole terms ago. Her mother had been really positive about the move from their old home after her divorce from Rachel's father. Rachel looked at her new school as a fresh start. She knew her parents' divorce had been difficult for them both and she wanted to make the move as easy as possible for her mother.

Rachel had tried her hardest to settle into her new school. She always handed her work in on time and she put all of her effort into making sure her work was completed to the best of her ability. Rachel had even joined the school's netball team. It was probably because of this that she had found it difficult to make friends. Rachel found that she had a natural talent for netball and her teacher replaced Sally, an enormous and nasty girl, with Rachel as team captain. Since then, Sally had done everything to make Rachel's life a misery. This even went as far as ringing her and shouting abuse down the phone.

In the above story, the writer uses the opening line as a starting point to explain what happened to Rachel when she began at a new school. There are, of course, plenty of other stories that could be written given this opening.

Now complete the following task:

+ **Write the first paragraph to your own story using the opening line: 'It was my first day at work and I had no idea what to expect ... '**

Alternatively, you might be given the ending sentence and asked to write the story that finishes with that line. The potential problem with this task is that you might forget to write the given line as your final sentence. Always check to make sure your story logically reaches an appropriate conclusion and then remember to add the given line to the end of your story.

2 Descriptive and imaginative writing

Read the following end to a story that finishes with the line '... *Just at that moment, I heard the car draw up outside and I knew I was in deep, deep trouble.*'

The party had been a great success. That was obvious from the way the house looked. There were empty cans everywhere and crisps and sweets had been trampled into mum's fluffy pink carpet. All over the lounge lay my drunken friends and people I'd never seen before! I hiccuped noisily as dad's cider began to take effect. Coats and shoes lay all over the place and as I walked towards the bathroom a hand grabbed my ankle, 'Excellent party, mate!' exclaimed Rob, right before he collapsed in a heap on the floor. I laughed to myself and thought, 'Well, we only finish our GCSEs once, don't we?' I was feeling very smug with myself that I had thrown the best party ever and mum and dad would never know that I'd broken all of their rules! Just at that moment, I heard the car draw up outside and I knew I was in deep, deep trouble.

This closing paragraph to the story shows how you must lead up to the closing line. Here, the writer has thrown a party and thinks he has got away with it. However, the end sentence shows that he hasn't!

Now complete the following tasks:
- **Write the final paragraph for a story that ends with the line: '... He picked up his bag and walked away without looking back.'**
- **Return to your group list of topics and titles, opening and closing lines. Choose one of them and write a full answer.**

Write about two sides of A4 paper under timed conditions in 40 minutes.

Exam tips

- Keep a cool head – make sure you show your very best standard of expression and organization in this task. Your handwriting, paragraphing and punctuation should come together to make a neat product.
- The standard of your writing should not deteriorate between the opening and the ending of the piece. If you are rather prone to error, then by writing too quickly and too much you will possibly quadruple the number of mistakes you make, which would be a disaster! Therefore, the better organized you are, the fewer mistakes you might make.
- You may not have a large vocabulary, but you can still suggest to the examiner that you have a thoughtful, developing range of words by avoiding the use of slang like 'brill' and 'cool' (except in dialogue).
- Make sure your writing is accurate. Be very careful with your basic skills and general presentation. Use Unit 2.3 at the end of this section to help you with your technical accuracy.

Controlling your narrative

It is very important that you give a clear impression to the examiner that you are in control of your writing.

- Before you start to write, think about how you might get the reader interested AND how you are going to develop and then end the narrative.
- Keep your feet on the ground – don't be too ambitious about the plot (the steps in the story) and the characterization. Limit yourself sensibly, by not writing complicated plot-driven adventures which end ridiculously. Also limit yourself to a small, manageable number of characters.
- Bring in descriptive skills to some extent, but don't overload with 'set-piece' well-practised settings or pen-portraits. Add touches of description naturally, at the points that the reader will be helped by a detail or two to visualize a character or a scene.
- Avoid gratuitous violence in your story. Don't give the impression that you love bloodthirsty description and action. Remember that your maturity is on the line in your writing, so don't be childish and don't show off!

2 Descriptive and imaginative writing

Technical accuracy in descriptive and imaginative writing

All of your descriptive and imaginative efforts will go to waste if you do not write accurately. You must consistently pay attention to technical accuracy on two fronts and try to:

a avoid careless errors

b improve your style.

In most pressurized situations, you should try to strike a balance between being reasonably ambitious and maintaining a good level of accuracy. It is understood that occasional errors will occur under pressure, but that is no excuse for failing to tackle any bad habits or weaknesses that you have in your writing.

In this unit you will have a quick refresher course on aspects of language that you need to take on board, particularly for imaginative and descriptive writing. The technical terms will be kept to a minimum and you will be pleased to know that you do not have to learn any of them to succeed in an exam! If they help you to tighten up your writing skills, they will have served their purpose.

Sentence structure

Read the following extracts from an authentic examination piece of descriptive writing on the subject of the January Sales. Look particularly at the variety of sentences.

They stand ready for battle. Shop assistants wait pensively, but the doors of Marks and Spencer still do not spring open. The shop windows are emblazoned with red and white signs: '50% off!' Security guards wait, ready to pounce. The manager puts the key in the lock, turns it slowly anti-clockwise, and takes the handle.

BANG! The battle has started! Hordes of people flood through the door and the noise level increases. Housewives are on a mission. They have had a tip off from the woman on the cosmetics stand who lives on Penarth Road that there are going to be some good offers in the lingerie department. Elbows sharpened, they are prepared to do anything to achieve their goals. Shop assistants run maniacally around the counters, wrapping up china, folding clothes, handing over bags. The till bells chime out over the shop floor, calling to the fresh, crisp bank notes ...

... A voice starts to boom over the tannoy system: 'Ladies,

may we interest you in a 75% reduction in the hosiery department, second floor?'

It is nearing four o'clock now. The assistants are sighing with sheer relief that the day is nearly at an end. Their skin has greyed and any plans for a drink after work have been ditched. The last tills chime. It is time to go home, as the announcements over the tannoy are subtly reminding customers that now they must leave. The last two women are ushered away through the door. The manager comes back with his key, puts it in the lock, turns it slowly clockwise and shuts the door.

In imaginative writing, you should vary your sentence structure in order to add interest to your writing. By varying the structure and length of sentences your writing will be more powerful, more dramatic and more interesting for the reader.

The heart of any sentence is the **verb**. A verb is a word (or a group of words) that indicates an action or a state of being. To help your awareness of verbs, they are printed in **bold** throughout the following grid.

Read about **simple**, **compound** and **complex sentences** as essential variations in any piece of writing. Consider the role of **noun phrases** in enriching the descriptive element of your writing. Note the concern about **minor sentences**.

TYPES OF SENTENCE OR PHRASE	EXAMPLES

Simple sentences

Simple sentences are part of every good writer's kit – just don't overdo them. Here, the variety of sentence openings helps the effect.

- *They **stand** ready for battle.*
- *The battle **has started**!*
- *Housewives **are** on a mission.*
- *It **is** nearing four o'clock now.*
- *The last tills **chime**.*

Compound sentences

Compound sentences, using the conjunctions 'and' or 'but', can be employed freely, provided you know where to stop each one! Avoid a long sequence, at all costs, of *and ... but ... but ... and ... .*

- *Shop assistants **wait** pensively, but the doors still do not spring open.*
- *The manager **puts** the key in the lock, **turns** it slowly anti-clockwise, and **takes** the handle.*
- *Hordes of people **flood** through the door and the noise level **increases**.*
- *The manager **comes back** with his key, **puts** it in the lock, **turns** it slowly clockwise and **shuts** the door.*

Complex sentences

Complex sentences join ideas together within the same sentence. You need to use this kind of sentence fairly commonly, or your writing will appear very limited.

REMEMBER The conjunctions 'if', 'when', 'as', 'although', 'so', 'that' ... feature as a key link word in many complex sentences.

The relative pronouns 'who', 'which', 'that', 'whom' act as linking words in complex sentences. So do present participles ('-ing' verb endings) and past participles ('-ed' verb endings).

- *They **have had** a tip off from the woman on the cosmetics stand <u>who</u> **lives** on Penarth Road <u>that</u> there **are going to be** some good offers in the lingerie department.*
- *Elbows **sharpen<u>ed</u>**, they **are prepared to do** anything **to achieve** their goals.*
- *Shop assistants **run** maniacally around the counters, **wrapping** up china, **folding** clothes, **handing** over bags.*
- *The assistants **are sighing** with sheer relief <u>that</u> the day **is** nearly at an end.*
- *It **is** time **to go** home, <u>as</u> the announcements over the tannoy **are** subtly **reminding** customers <u>that</u> now they **must leave**.*

Noun phrases

(including extended noun phrases)

A noun phrase is a group of words constructed around a noun (or pronoun). It expands the meaning of that noun (or pronoun).

- *red and white signs: '50% off.'*
- *a tip off from the woman on the cosmetics stand*
- *some good offers in the lingerie department*
- *the fresh, crisp bank notes ...*

These are the staple diet of descriptive and imaginative writing, the nouns and adjectives that bring a piece of writing to life.

Minor sentences

A minor sentence is one with no verb or with an incomplete verb. The only example of a minor sentence in the feature text above is 'Bang!'. The writer might however have written: *Ready for battle ... Housewives on a mission.*

This might work as a deliberate attempt to shorten sentences for dramatic effect, but if the following had been written, the writer's understanding of sentence structure might be open to doubt.
Ready for battle. Shop assistants waiting pensively.
Housewives on a mission. Hordes of shoppers flooding through the doors.

WARNING Do not get stuck in a sequence of minor sentences. Note how they can appear to reduce the sense of action in a scene.

> See Unit 4.3 (Technical accuracy in transactional and discursive writing) for further support in **sentence structure**, relating to:
> - more complex sentences
> - the passive voice
> - indirect (or reported) speech
> - connectives and conjunctions.

Now complete this task:

- **Write an opening paragraph (or two) in response to the title 'Another Time, Another Place'.**

Treat the task as an imaginative writing challenge, but try to integrate some descriptive quality into the opening. Above all, concentrate on using a range of sentence types – simple, compound, complex.

Punctuation

In imaginative writing, the most effective way of commanding your reader's attention is through correct punctuation. This means understanding the basic rules for using full stops, capital letters, commas, question marks, exclamation marks and speech marks. Some of the rules are more flexible than others and require your personal judgement about controlling the pace of your writing. The basic rules need to be observed, though – without argument in most cases! Read through the grid to remind yourselves about basic punctuation.

PUNCTUATION	EXAMPLES

Full stops

There are no excuses for not using them and no excuses for not getting them right most of the time! Using full stops correctly is tied in with understanding simple, compound and complex sentences. In exam terms, it's a disaster if you cannot use full stops reliably – full stop!

- *Hordes of people flood through the door and the noise level increases. Housewives are on a mission.*
- *It is nearing four o'clock now. The assistants are sighing with sheer relief that the day is nearly at an end. Their skin has greyed and any plans for a drink after work have been ditched. The last tills chime.*

Capital letters

This is not really a book that is intended to teach you about capital letters, but, if you are shaky in this area, read on!

a Check that you are sure what the upper case or capital form of each letter is. You send out a bad signal if you write upper case letters in the middle of words (e.g. woRds) or if your capitals are no bigger than your lower case letters (e.g. mr sam camman).

b Use a capital letter for the first letter of a sentence (after a full stop) and for the first letter of each word of a name.

c Capital letters are also used to indicate shouting or any other loud noise.

- *A voice starts to boom over the tannoy system: 'Ladies, may we interest you ... ?'*
- *January*
- *Marks and Spencer*
- *Penarth Road*
- *BANG!*

2 Descriptive and imaginative writing

Commas

Commas can be a little tricky because you often have to use your judgement and ask yourself – 'Is a pause within this sentence helpful here?' Using commas between sentences, instead of full stops, is normally a sign of poor sentence structure as well as poor punctuation.

♠ *Shop assistants wait pensively, but the doors of Marks and Spencer still do not spring open.*

♠ *Elbows sharpened, they are prepared to do anything to achieve their goals.*

Commas are markers between items in lists and between phrases and clauses (key groups of words) within a sentence.

♠ *The till bells chime out over the shop floor, calling to the fresh, crisp bank notes …*

So you have some choice as to when you use commas – modern writers tend to favour a 'light' use of the comma.

Question marks

Not normally a problem, though some writers are careless and miss them out.

'Ladies, may we interest you in a 75% reduction in the hosiery department, second floor?'

Exclamation marks

Quite a favourite with many students!!!! However, avoid this kind of overdose of exclamation marks because they will quickly lose any effect.

♠ *BANG!*

♠ *The battle has started!*

Speech marks

Dialogue, conversation and speech give you an opportunity to show that you can use speech marks. Make sure you take advantage of that opportunity.

♠ *'Ladies, may we interest you in a 75% reduction in the hosiery department, second floor?'*

REMEMBER Speech marks surround the precise words spoken by a character.

See Unit 4.3 (Technical accuracy in transactional and discursive writing) for further support in **punctuation**, relating to:
♠ paragraphs
♠ more about commas
♠ apostrophes
♠ semi-colons
♠ colons
♠ brackets
♠ dashes.

Now complete the following task:

♣ **Copy the following piece of writing and punctuate it replacing each oblique line (/) with either a full stop or a comma.**

When you choose a full stop, make sure you use a capital letter to start the following sentence.

She sat in the waiting room / clutching a cup of coffee / her face was pale and her eyes looked tired / she was staring ahead of her as though she was in a trance / all around her / people were talking / babies were crying and / in the distance / an ambulance siren could be heard / she didn't seem to notice.

Several times in the night she woke up in a cold sweat / finally / she decided not to sleep and instead sat on a chair / looking out of the window and thinking of things like her shopping list and if she could afford to go on holiday next year / she thought about everything except Adrian / the accident and her terrifying nightmares / a light knock on the door interrupted her thought / she looked up and saw / Doctor Lowe enter / his face was grave and his deep eyes looked tired /

'No /' she thought / 'please no /'

He opened his mouth to say the words she was dreading / suddenly / he broke into a wide smile /

'He's awake /'

Now complete the following task, practising your own punctuation:

♣ **Write the opening paragraph (or two) in response to the title 'A Day in the Country'.**

You can treat this as either a descriptive task or as a narrative (imaginative) task. Concentrate particularly on your control and range of punctuation, using all of the items covered above, including speech marks.

Spelling

Poor spelling detracts from the story you are telling or the scene you are describing. To make your writing interesting, you should use a range of words – simple and complex. However, some simple words are often misspelled or confused with similar sounding words. These are known as 'homophones' and using the incorrect homophone can dramatically alter the meaning of your writing. For example: 'The orange buoy floated in the sea' has a very different meaning to 'the orange boy floated in the sea'. Read the notes in the grid on the next page to help you with your spelling.

Homophones

Homophones are words that are spelled differently, but which sound the same (or very similar). If you confuse *no* and *know*, or *to, too* and *two*, or *there, their* and *they're*, then you need to take stock and work at your spelling with some purpose.

- ♠ ... *Ready <u>for</u> battle*
- ♠ *Shop assistants <u>wait</u> ...*
- ♠ <u>*Hordes*</u> *of people ...*
- ♠ ... <u>*through*</u> *the door*
- ♠ ... <u>*there*</u> *are going <u>to</u> <u>be</u> ...*
- ♠ ... *achieve <u>their</u> goals*
- ♠ ... *the shop <u>floor</u>*
- ♠ ... <u>*sheer*</u> *relief*
- ♠ ... <u>*wrapping*</u> *up china*

Vowel choices

You have to learn to group words and to treat some as exceptions to a rule or part of a very small group.

- ♠ *r<u>ea</u>dy*
- ♠ *prep<u>a</u>red*
- ♠ *n<u>ea</u>ring*
- ♠ *g<u>u</u>ards*
- ♠ *incr<u>ea</u>ses*
- ♠ *reli<u>e</u>f*
- ♠ *l<u>ea</u>ve*
- ♠ *cust<u>o</u>mers*

Double consonants

You should expect a short vowel sound before a double consonant, e.g. *wrapping*.

- ♠ *ba<u>tt</u>le*
- ♠ *a<u>ss</u>istants*
- ♠ *a<u>nn</u>ouncements*
- ♠ *ta<u>nn</u>oy*
- ♠ *wra<u>pp</u>ing*

Irregular plurals

The regular plural in English is -s, as in *bags*. (Do not use an apostrophe for a straightforward plural!).

WARNING Irregular plurals appear in common words – witness the examples on the right.

- ♠ *lad<u>ies</u>*
- ♠ *w<u>o</u>men*
- ♠ *housewi<u>ves</u>*
- ♠ *cloth<u>es</u>*

Word endings

Fairly basic, in truth. Verb endings (e.g. -ed) and adverb endings (e.g. -ly, -ally) figure prominently as areas of weakness in students' spelling.

- ♠ *pensive<u>ly</u>*
- ♠ *maniac<u>ally</u>*
- ♠ *ditch<u>ed</u>*
- ♠ *usher<u>ed</u>*
- ♠ *hand<u>le</u>*

Silent letters

Many words with silent letters have an interesting history, dating back to a time when they were NOT silent!

- ♠ *su<u>b</u>tly*
- ♠ *si<u>g</u>hing*
- ♠ <u>*w*</u>*rapping*
- ♠ *throu<u>g</u>h*
- ♠ *int<u>e</u>rest*

Polysyllabic words

Polysyllabic words are generally regarded as words of three or more syllables (*poly* = much, many). An awareness of syllables will help you spell these words correctly.

- ♠ *hosiery*
- ♠ *security*
- ♠ *lingerie*
- ♠ *manager*

See Unit 4.3 (Technical accuracy in transactional and discursive writing) for a second opportunity to explore areas of **spelling**.

Now complete the following task:

♣ **Return to the two pieces of writing that you have attempted in this unit:**
   Another Time, Another Place
   A Day in the Country
   a **Establish which spellings are wrong. Correct them and work out the area(s) of your spelling weakness(es) from the grid on page 63.**
   b **Analyse your correct spelling. Write down the headings from the grid on page 63 and compile examples of correct spelling under each heading.**

Grammar

Grammar is a further area that needs your attention for technical accuracy in writing. This will be covered in more detail in Unit 4.3.

Quickly correct these errors of agreement.
We was ..., I seen ..., ... more better, Do your worstest, We done good, It ain't no good, ... it's been one of them days.

See Unit 4.3 (Technical accuracy in transactional and discursive writing) for further support in **grammar**, relating to:
♣ pronouns
♣ comparatives and superlatives
♣ prepositions
♣ agreement
♣ verbs.

Unfortunately, if you write carelessly, without concentration, or you simply hurry and panic in an exam, your work will be very disappointing. Could any of the pieces on pages 65 and 66 be yours?

2 Descriptive and imaginative writing

Complete the following task:

♣ **Discuss the weaknesses of each of the following pieces of writing. Re-write each of them, correcting the errors *and* improving the vocabulary and style.**

1

It was my first day at work and I had no idea what to expect but this is what happened. I was mean't to be in work by 7:00AM. But I over slept and got in at 7:45AM. So I had already started bad and it was'nt even 9:00 in the morning. So I was mean't to go out with the lorry drive. But he had give up waiting for me and gone. So I had nobody to work with now.

2

"Are you going again Saturday?" She asked "No, I'm probably baby sitting for this one!" I replied! But as I placed my hand on Josh head where's Josh, I cried I couldn't see him anywhere, I sprinted up and down the aisle, my heart was pounding and sweat dripped from my forehead. I have never been so paniced in my life suddenly everything went black and nothing made sense. I took a few deep breathes and wiped the sweat from my brow but still Josh was nowhere in sight.

3

When a market is busy it is just full of people, it is realy loud because all you can hear is people talking and the music from the stalls. When you want to look at a stall it is very hard because there is so many people trying to look and buy at once and you are just pushed out of the way. All you can see is people pushing each other and trying to look at things on the stall. There are a lot of stalls at the market such as people selling clothes, jewelly, fruit and vegetables, toys and antiques and many many more.

4

The park was very busy today, I even said so to a passer-by which I didn't no. The sun was directly above the common and the heat rays were beaming down tiny balls of sweat were already beginning to form on my slightly tanned skin. The tan which after today would definately improve. In the end it did improve but not to the extent of which I would have liked.

5

I rember my experiance as if it was yesterday, the day had started out like any other, I woke up, showerd, and dressed, ate as usual. It was quiet a sunny day and so I took the newspaper in the garden to read, I sat down by the pool and thought that the garden looked more vibrant than ever before.

6

the beach, everybody loves the beach. Except my grandma but then I don't think she likes anything. It seems to sum up everything that is good and hot. In fact I would say it sums up summer. I never met noone whom doesn't like the summer except my grandma.

7

suddenly the phone went dead, oh I hate mobiles, I thought to myself, everyones got one but the always cut out or the one person in the world you want get hold of as their phone turned off. You know the other thing I hate more than anything. Hard butter. I cannot stand it. You cook your toast, get the knife out, and the butter wont cut.

Exam tips

- Think and plan (in your head) before you write.
- Write to the recommended length for each task, but don't go beyond it. Quality, not quantity!
- Do not use 'text speak' in your writing, e.g. cu.
- Do not be afraid to use a word that you cannot spell. If it is the right word or the best word for the occasion, use it.
- Check your work at the end of each task for silly errors.

2 Descriptive and imaginative writing

Non-fiction and media reading

Section A (Reading:15%) will test through structured questions the reading of non-fiction and media texts. Non-fiction texts may include: factsheets, leaflets, letters, extracts from autobiographies, biographies, diaries. Media texts may include: advertisements, reports and articles from newspapers, magazines, brochures. These two categories will usually be represented by separate texts (e.g. leaflet plus advertisement). Visual material will always be included in the material used.*

The reading skills required in responding to non-fiction and media texts are, on occasions, significantly different from those needed for the study of a literary text.

In 'real life' texts, you are often, as the reader, searching for information; the writer, meanwhile, may be trying to tempt you to buy something or to change your mind. In other respects, the main criteria being assessed are still:
*   location and reorganization – finding things and using your own words
*   inference – reading 'between the lines'
*   appreciation of style – looking at the way the writer writes.

This section of the book contains four units:

3.1 Locating details You will learn how to retrieve information.

3.2 Explaining and summarizing You will learn how to reorganize the text in your own words to show understanding.

3.3 Analysing persuasive techniques You will learn how to examine in detail the methods of selling ideas and products.

3.4 Comparing non-fiction and media texts You will learn how to compare, contrast and evaluate the treatment of a subject by looking at two different texts.

* The texts used in Units 1, 2 and 3 of this section have been specially written for the purpose of focusing on the reading skills covered by the respective units. The texts used in Unit 4 are authentic pairs of texts set alongside each other for comparative purposes.

According to the article, what are the attractions and benefits of ___ ?

According to the factsheet, what are the effects of ___ ?

List the reasons why ___ , according to the leaflet.

Finding information in a text is the most basic of reading skills. However, the best readers occasionally slip up when asked to find straightforward facts and details. Likewise, if you are not a strong reader in other respects, you can still operate successfully by searching and finding key things.

When searching for information, it is important that you find more than the minimum amount. Whether it be items, reasons, excuses or problems, expand your list as fully as you can. In fact, a list is the logical means of collecting your information.

Read the article below taken from a Staffordshire guide.

Alton Towers – Staffordshire Pride

Alton Towers is perhaps the most famous theme park in Great Britain. Located in the heart of Staffordshire, it has plenty to offer children and adults alike. The park is divided into eleven separate "zones", each with a different theme. These include: Katanga Canyon, the home of the Congo Rapids and Runaway Train; Merrie England, where you'll find the Log Flume and spinning Tea Cups; and the Forbidden Valley, where you can ride the zero gravity roller coaster – Nemesis – if you dare.

Alton Towers is notorious for its death-defying roller coasters and every few years a new addition is constructed at the park – each one more terrifying than the last. 2002 saw the opening of AIR, reportedly the world's first horizontal roller coaster. You are belted into the seats and your legs are firmly strapped down. Then the carriages are tilted 90 degrees so that you seem to be lying on your stomach. This is the perfect position for flying and as the ride takes off this is what you feel like you are actually doing.

If you can brave AIR, then perhaps you should also try the other coasters the park has to offer. Oblivion is a vertical drop roller coaster where, once strapped in, you stare down hundreds of feet into a black smoking hole in the ground. Before you can properly take in the view, you are plummeting towards the hole – face first! It's all over in a flash, but what an unforgettable experience – to stare into Oblivion and come out the other side unscathed! If you still want more, then why not try the Black Hole – a roller coaster than runs its course completely in the dark. You have no idea what is coming next and all you can do is scream!

In addition to these there is also the Towers manor house itself and the extensive landscaped gardens that surround it. These are perfect for mums and dads who wish to escape from their excitable children for a while.

When you're tired of all that, why not retire to one of the many coffee shops or restaurants that the park has to offer, which include both fast food and traditional British menus? Alternatively, why not spend some time (and money!) browsing around the gift shops on Towers Street? There you'll find the perfect souvenirs to help you remember your wonderful day at the park.

Now answer the following question:

* **Name ten things from the article that would attract a visitor especially to Alton Towers.**

Write your answer either as a vertical list or as a reasonably short paragraph with your points made distinctly.

Before you dismiss the task as being too easy, stop and think! How do you make ten distinct points so that it is clear which attractions you are naming?

Do not simply copy out the bulk of the first paragraph:

The park is divided into eleven separate "zones", each with a different theme. These include: Katanga Canyon, the home of the Congo Rapids and Runaway Train; Merrie England ...

Do not copy the same thing twice:

... the zero-gravity roller coaster; Nemesis ...

Do not choose the items you can find anywhere:

... fast food; souvenirs ...

Read the following advertisement for Legoland.

Legoland is one of the first theme parks to be based around a popular children's toy. The whole park is dedicated to Lego and everything inside the park is made from plastic blocks of various sizes. Located in Windsor, the park has plenty to offer people, including eight different areas, each with its own theme. These range from Miniland, where you can witness the world in miniature, including the pyramids of Egypt and even a replica of Big Ben, to the Imagination Centre, where you can let your creativity flow and experiment with a range of models and designs made out of Lego.

If this isn't enough, then why not try passing your driving test in the Lego driving school after having a quick lesson on the Highway Code? Even the cars here are made out of Lego! Alternatively, you could try flying a hot air balloon on a ride that allows you to control the height and speed of your aircraft. For younger adventurers, there is Lego Explore Land, the home of the Ultimate Challenge, where you race down a water chute on a raft. It's in Explore Land that you'll also find Waterworks, Fairy Tale Brook and Playtown, all dedicated to family fun.

But don't think that Legoland doesn't have its fair share of rides. Why not try Space Tower or the Dragon Coaster or even Pirate Falls if you think you're brave enough? When all of the excitement gets too much, why not escape to one of the four restaurants the park has to offer, ranging from sea food to a typical fast food diner? There are also plenty of shops to explore, offering a great choice of gifts for the people back at home who missed out on your wonderful day at the park.

Now answer the following question:

* **According to the advert, what attractions can you expect to see at Legoland?**

TIP Location questions in exams generally expect you to search for ten answers and to write them down efficiently, in a list if you wish.

Information retrieval tasks are not always quite so straightforward. The type of text may be completely different from that in a theme park brochure and the style of question may be different too.

http://miroslav.com/view

Back Forward Stop Refresh Home AutoFill Print Mail Larger Smaller Preferences

Address: http://miroslav.com/view

The Internet – for and against

The Internet is now widely available and most people are connected to it via a modem on their home computer. This means that most people can have ready access to the extensive information available online. It is guaranteed that no matter how obscure the topic, someone somewhere will have created a website about it. Naturally this means that students can have full access to any information that may help with their school or college work. However, the convenience of the Internet also brings the problem of some students abusing this system and handing in work that has simply been downloaded off the web. It has been argued that the Internet is still only widely available to the rich, with many unemployed people still being unable to afford access. However, the planned introduction of Internet cafés in poorer areas or areas of high unemployment should solve this problem.

The Internet has opened up a whole new world to people who may not otherwise have the opportunity to socialise. Individuals who work unsociable hours can now converse with people all over the world. Chat rooms have been organised where you can talk about any topic you wish with people who share the same interests as you. The downside of this has been highlighted recently in the newspapers, however. Although most people who use chat rooms are genuine, there are some who prey on innocent and naïve users and take advantage of them. This is particularly true for young children, who may not know exactly who they are chatting with. The use of nicknames and usernames enables people to adopt a new persona online and, since most chat rooms are largely unregulated, there is the potential for misuse of this system too.

A recent development is that it is now possible to download music and movies from the Internet. However, this has been challenged by both the music and film industries because they claim that these downloads are illegal and are depriving their industries of money that rightly belongs to them.

For those people without a home computer, most companies now offer their employees the use of the Internet at work and through an Intranet (an internal company web) they have their own email address. There is the potential here for our traditional postal service to become obsolete because emailing is faster and more efficient. Paperwork and images can be sent to clients and friends within seconds, rather than within days. But email also causes difficulties. Computers can be temperamental at times and files can be lost in the vast expanse of cyberspace. Email is not convenient for those documents that require a signature nor can attachments be sent via recorded delivery to guarantee that they will be received.

Internet zone

Now answer the following question, by compiling the information clearly in two lists:

♣ **According to the passage, identify five advantages and five disadvantages of using the Internet.**

Check as you proceed that you have expressed each point clearly.

Five advantages of using the Internet, according to the passage, are:

1. _____
2. _____
3. _____
4. _____
5. _____

Five disadvantages of using the Internet, according to the passage, are:

1. _____
2. _____
3. _____
4. _____
5. _____

In this example, you must try to identify the ten points required by the question: five advantages and five disadvantages. The key to succeeding with this question is to ensure that you give exactly what is being asked for.

Read the following article about *Operation Christmas Child*. As you read, identify five gifts that can be sent to the children of Eastern Europe and five gifts that cannot be sent.

OPERATION CHRISTMAS CHILD

Operation Christmas Child is organised and run by the Salvation Army. Its aim is to deliver boxes of presents to children in countries that are split by war or famine and send to them a message of hope from Britain. To take part in this project all you have to do is to find an average sized shoebox and cover it with Christmas wrapping paper. Then fill the box with presents and take it to your local Kwik Fit garage or Salvation Army shop and they will send it on. Do not wrap any presents individually. There are some rules and regulations about what can and cannot be sent in the shoeboxes.

The first thing you need to do is decide who your box will be for, a boy or a girl, then decide what you will put into it. The children always need hygiene-based products, such as toothbrushes, toothpaste, soap and flannels. But you should avoid including anything that is liquid based, such as bubble bath or shampoo, because these might spill over all of the other presents in the box. Clothes can also be sent, but these must be small enough to fit inside the box. As a rule, restrict clothing to hats, scarves, gloves or caps. You can include some small sweets or lollipops but ensure they are well within the use-by date as parcels take a while to reach their destination. For this reason you should avoid including any crisps, biscuits or cakes.

Toys can also be included, such as a teddy bear, a puzzle or jigsaw, or trucks and cars. But you should not include any toy that is war-related, such as guns or knives, for obvious reasons. Do not send any books with words in or any toy with complicated instructions. Finally, you may wish to include a greetings card or photo of yourself for the child.

Now answer the following question:

- **Identify five types of gift that can be sent to the children of Eastern Europe and five types of gift that cannot be sent.**

You should take no longer than 10–15 minutes on this question.

Take care that you do not just copy out a list of items that are essentially the same **type** of gift.

Exam tips

- Do not treat a location (search and find) question lightly. Concentrate and make every effort to find the points.
- Answer this type of question in a vertical list OR in an efficient paragraph with items clearly separated.
- Do not write explanations where they are not needed or expected!
- This kind of question, requiring you to retrieve information, will not necessarily be the first question on the paper.
- The 'question' may actually start with a command, like 'List ...'. On other occasions it will begin 'What are ...?' Be alert to the wording of questions.
- This is not a general knowledge test. Take your information from your reading of the text, not from your personal experience of the topic.

Unit 3.2 Explaining and summarizing

What impressions does this newspaper article create of ____ ?

What are the writer's attitudes to ____ ?

What kind of person is this advertisement aimed at? What evidence can you find to support your views?

What does the writer say to defend ____ ?

These questions ask you to use the information you have been given and form it into one response. You may be asked to reflect on the writer's attitudes or point of view or you may be asked to explain who the audience is.

The key to these questions is always to support your comments with evidence from the text. This may mean using short quotations effectively and appropriately by integrating them into your writing. It may also mean 'echoing' the text by using your own words for explaining the meaning of the writer's words. Do not make statements without referring to the text.

A question that asks about the attitudes **of the writer** does **not** normally require you to reveal **your** attitude.

Explaining requires you to disentangle ideas and viewpoints from a text and to rewrite them as far as possible in your own words. You should do this in a way that communicates clearly to the reader and in such a way that leaves no doubt that you have understood the text.

Any question referring to attitude and audience will need an answer that 'explains' rather than simply 'lists' some points.

Summarizing is the skill of picking out the main points of a text in answer to a question and drawing them together, sometimes to work out an overall attitude and show an 'overview' understanding.

Attitude means a way of thinking about someone or something, in other words a point of view, a belief, an opinion.

You should always focus on the text and identify relevant information that supports your comments. Then you must express your response carefully, sentence by sentence, making sure that your writing is logical and clear, and can stand up to reasonably close investigation.

P Plates!

Putting yourself on probation has its benefits

It's a feeling that stays with you forever. That wonderful moment when you sit behind the wheel and notice that for the first time the passenger seat isn't occupied by an instructor or an examiner. You've passed your driving test and those L plates are a thing of the past.

But as even the most competent of drivers would have to admit, it can feel as though you're being thrown in at the deep end. Statistics also reveal that you are more likely to have an accident in your first two years of driving than you are at any other point in your driving career. Indeed, in 2000 17–19 year olds made up just 4% of all licence holders, but were involved in 10% of accidents.

So what can you do to ease your way into a long and safe driving career? For the past ten years many newly qualified drivers have chosen to swap their red L plates for green P (Probation) plates once they have passed their test. Available from car accessory centres, they let other road users know that you have recently passed your test and that you're on a steep learning curve that every driver has to climb after qualifying for a full licence.

At present, there are no official requirements for drivers who pass their test in Great Britain to display P plates on their car after they have passed their test. However, the Government encourages their use by newly qualified drivers and is seeking their views on making them compulsory.

Although the voluntary set-up in Great Britain is still in its infancy other countries use similar schemes, including Spain, France, Finland, Japan and Australia. A mandatory probation period already exists in Northern Ireland. Under the R Driver scheme, all newly qualified drivers are required to display red R (Restricted) plates for a full year after passing their test. The plates are of similar design and style to the traditional L plates and signify to other road users that the driver has been driving for less than a year.

The scheme also restricts drivers to a maximum speed of 45mph. Similar experiments in other countries have brought encouraging results. In Austria, for example, the introduction in 1992 of a two-year probationary period for new drivers saw accident rates fall by 32%. Similarly, newly qualified drivers in Norway were up to 50% less likely to have an accident after the Government introduced a two-year probation scheme.

To **P** or not to P?

Swapping your L plates for P plates isn't the only way in which you can smooth the transition between learner and full licence holder. The Pass Plus scheme – backed by the Driving Standards Agency – is designed to equip drivers with the kind of day to day skills that would otherwise take years to acquire. The course consists of six sessions that include driving at night, driving on motorways and driving in-town.

What's more, there's no nerve-wracking test at the end of the course. If your instructor is satisfied with your overall performance, you receive a certificate from the DSA which could entitle you to a handy discount on your insurance policy.

> In 2000 17–19 year olds made up just 4% of all licence holders, but were involved in 10% of accidents

Now answer the question:

- **What does the writer say to support the use of P plates in Great Britain?**

Think about:
- the reasons for using P plates
- the arguments for making P plates compulsory, not voluntary
- who the article is aimed at
- the use of facts and figures
- the references to other countries.

Do not simply write down a 'knee-jerk' answer – for example:

The article is aimed at people who use P plates. The reasons that the writer supports the use of P plates is because it says 'In 2000 17–19 year-olds made up just 4% of all licence holders, but were involved in 10% of accidents.'

This is a poor answer because:

1   A moment's thought will tell you that people who already use P plates are not the main target audience for this article.
2   The supporting evidence is one long quotation lifted from outside the main body of text. The quotation does not *explain* a reason for using P plates any more than it does for *not* using P plates. It does no explaining, but leaves it to the reader to do the work!
3   In any case, neither part of the answer is extended beyond one sentence, so the mark awarded in an exam would be low.

Use a grid like the one below to help you build an answer using all of the bullet points.

POINTS TO CONSIDER	COMMENT
Reasons for using P plates	
Argumentsfor making P plates compulsory	
Who the article is aimed at	
Use of facts and figures	
References to other countries	

Read the following article about reality television. This type of programme (for example, *Popstars*, *Big Brother*) has been popular in recent years, both with viewers and large numbers of people who wish to take part in a wide variety of challenges that expose them to the close scrutiny of the public. Consider the views of the writer.

ArtificialReality

★ Reality television has a lot to answer for. Over the past few years, it has given us Darius, Jade Goody, Nasty Nick Bateman and countless other instantly forgettable wannabes. These individuals lay themselves open to ridicule and scrutiny by applying to take part in the television shows and then criticise the media and the public in general for not taking them seriously. Anyone in these shows must realise that they have a very limited shelf life. The public shows a huge interest in them at the beginning but by the end of the tedious ten-week run of Big Brother most people couldn't care less who wins. It's always amazing when the presenters announce that they have received over a million phone votes on eviction night. I suspect the viewers have their phones firmly set to redial.

★ As if temporarily making nobodies into somebodies wasn't bad enough, television producers, in their ultimate wisdom, have seen fit to make ex-somebodies back into somebodies again. We now have Celebrity Big Brother, where you can watch once-famous Z-list celebs have nervous breakdowns on live television, and I'm a Celebrity Get Me Out of Here, where celebrities hanging on the fringe of fame are left in the heart of the Australian bush. The only drawback with the latter show is that the celebrities are brought back to Britain when the show is over. Shows such as these enable these former celebs to climb back up the fame list; I understand they are classed as Y-list celebs now.

★ There are rumours from across the ocean that American television bosses are lining up more and more outrageous reality television programmes. Then again, the idea of couples fighting for the chance to divorce on national television does not seem so bizarre when you consider that this has been developed in America – the country that has given us The Osbournes. Whoever would have thought that both sides of the Atlantic would have been gripped by the antics of Ozzy Osbourne and his Addams-like family? And now, more recently, Anna Nicole Smith. Until her show, she was only ever famous for marrying an eighty-five year old billionaire … for love. Suggestions that the family's antics are rigged have of course been strenuously denied, but you can't help wondering if anyone really behaves like that and, if they do, should it really be on television? The only question that remains is, how much lower can reality television go?

3 Non-fiction and media reading

Now answer the following question:

🔹 **What impressions of reality television shows does the writer of this article create?**

Here are some central comments about the writer's attitude that may reassure you that you are on the right lines, but they are not quite focused on the above question. Once again, you need to position yourself to write an effective answer. Ask yourself: 'Does the writer create a good (favourable) or bad (unfavourable) impression of the shows?' You might choose to reword some comments below to make a really focused response.

The writer is against Reality Television shows. The writer does not agree with making unknown people into celebrities and agrees even less with the idea of using celebrities in these programmes. The writer refers to the stars of these shows as "instantly forgettable" and "nobodies", which clearly shows that he/she disapproves of them. The writer also implies that the shows do not have many viewers, only a handful who ring repeatedly on eviction night and make it look like the show has a large audience, "I suspect the viewers have their phones firmly set to redial". The writer is even harsher when it comes to former celebrities starring in these shows, saying that they move from being Z-list celebs to being Y-list. This is a sarcastic comment that implies that these people are really still only former celebrities, even after they have participated in these shows.

In answering the question, take up some of the points in the paragraph above and work them into your answer. Start your response with a clear answer to the question, then add and amend your explanations and evidence as you proceed. Find three more quotations (words, phrases, maybe a whole sentence) that fit in with the thrust of your answer.

REMEMBER Your own opinion of Reality TV is not the one that counts here, though there may be some scope for implied criticism of the writer, if you take the view that the writer is being unfair to these programmes.

It may help you to build an answer if you take on board impressions given of the different components of Reality TV: the production, the presenters, the participants, the viewers.

Now read the following extracts from a longer account in which a Cardiff City and Wales football fan, Mark Ainsbury, shares his experiences of his trip to Baku, the capital of Azerbaijan, to watch Wales.

An appreciation of the writer's point of view or attitude is critical to being able to understand any text, especially perhaps when it is a piece of travel writing. Often in travel writing, the writer is cast in the role of trying to explain an unusual experience, largely by describing it.

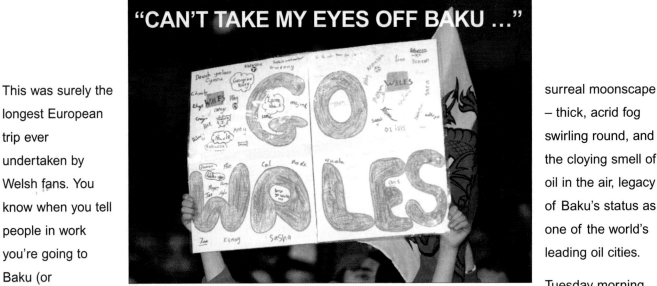

"CAN'T TAKE MY EYES OFF BAKU ..."

This was surely the longest European trip ever undertaken by Welsh fans. You know when you tell people in work you're going to Baku (or Hartlepool) for a football match, and they look at you with that patronising face that says "you sad, dysfunctional fool", Ha, well, little do they know, we have the secret of eternal youth and happiness. Well, happiness, at least. Azerbaijan sounded so far, we just had to go…

We all knew Azerbaijan away was the key game in the campaign for Wales, and the 8-hour flight via Istanbul gave us plenty of time to ponder the enormity of the task, while we checked the alarmist list of Baku Do's and Don'ts given to us on the plane. Don't go out alone at night, don't talk to anyone, that kind of stuff. Yeah, right, I've had scarier times in Mothercare. Little did we know we would end up having the time of our lives and the friendliest welcome (and by far the very worst drivers anywhere, ever) that this reporter has had in 30+ Wales away trips. Touching down in Baku in the middle of the night was like walking into the middle of a surreal moonscape – thick, acrid fog swirling round, and the cloying smell of oil in the air, legacy of Baku's status as one of the world's leading oil cities.

Tuesday morning let us snatch back a couple of the 4 hours stolen from us by the time difference, before an early date with the assembled masses of BBC TV, Radio Wales and Radio 5 Live waiting for us on the steps of our hotel. After years of travelling around the less prosperous fringes of Europe just to watch our country play football, a few Wales fans had the idea that we would do fundraising work for local orphanages in Baku, to at least make a small difference to some kids while we were out there. The media had picked up on this and came with us on the Tuesday morning to the first 2 orphanages, hauntingly named Number 1 and Number 16, a legacy of the 8000 kids orphaned in Baku alone by the recent war with neighbouring Armenia. The kids at the orphanages were delighted as we turned up, and couldn't get enough of the Wales shirts, footballs, complete kits, toys, and signed pictures of Giggsy, Matthew Jones and, er, Robert Page we took for them.

3 Non-fiction and media reading

The Heads of the orphanages were fulsome in their praise of the Welsh fans' efforts, as no away fans had ever gone to Baku before, and certainly no-one had ever been to visit them to bring things for the kids. As the TV and radio interviewed us about the initiative, the kids played up for the cameras by roundly thrashing us at an impromptu kickaround in their playground. So much for bloody charity.

The trip to the Tofig Bahramov stadium for the main game (named after the Azeri linesman who invented a goal in '66 so England could win the World Cup) was on organised coaches, which took us through some of the less salubrious areas of the city. This gave us the first real feeling that a lot of Baku residents are really struggling, as the transition to a free market economy leaves behind those less able to make money from private enterprise (that all sounds a bit Newsnight, sorry). The main part of the city was surprisingly affluent and laid back, certainly compared with its Armenian and Moldovan equivalents, but out of the centre there were whole families living in shells of buildings, huddled round small fires for warmth, and us just there for a football match.

The relative lack of excitement on the pitch (Wales fans not killing themselves with nerves) meant we could relax. The 60s'-style rattle I had taken with me got confiscated by the police, but was given back once they had examined it to see how it worked, like as if I had brought a fully-functioning alien to the match. The police could not have been nicer, and Wales fans wandering around the stadium at half time were met only with friendliness, the ubiquitous greeting of 'Ryan Giggs' and general wonder (or ridicule) at the fact that we were wearing Wales flags as skirts.

The charity work done by the Wales fans goes on. We are setting up a registered charity and doing a similar thing when we go to Belgrade for children there, as well as trying to fund the Azeri children from the orphanage who did the dancing to visit the Eisteddfod in Llangollen. Anyone interested in helping or contributing to Wales fans' ongoing fundraising please email Mark.

Now answer the following question:
♠ **What are the writer's attitudes to Azerbaijan?**

To build a response, you might consider the following:
- the distance
- the journey
- the airport
- the orphanages and the children
- the city
- the police
- the crowd.

Take note of the plural 'attitudes' (not 'attitude') in the question and consider the changes and variations of attitude that take place on a trip to a different country – i.e. what you're expecting compared with what you get.

Thinking Green – Seeing Red

The latest conservation initiative is to encourage people to transfer their good "green" habits from the home to the workplace. It seems it's not enough to be recycling at home, we are now being made to feel guilty for spending all of our time in work doing our jobs! Although conserving the planet is clearly a good thing and has very obvious benefits, we are constantly being made to feel guilty for putting our wheelie bins out each week. We seem to be driven to the point of going through our rubbish each week to ensure that a stray piece of lettuce leaf hasn't slipped into the bins instead of into the compost heap. As if this isn't enough we are now expected to transfer all of these neurotic behaviours to the workplace, previously a place for escape from obsessing about recycling.

It seems it is not enough to have to deal with computers that continually crash, workmates that do less than their fair share and bosses who impose unreasonable deadlines. We are now expected to remember not to throw a single piece of paper into the bin, but to put it into a recycling box. We are also expected to car-share to and from work. The idea of seeing certain David Brent-like workmates at the office is bad enough, but the thought of being trapped in a car with them during rush hour is not appealing. Tempers get frayed when loved-ones are in the car; what would it be like with three or four people you detest?

Another suggestion is to reduce the amount of electricity used in businesses. That would certainly solve one problem – at least if the electricity was off, millions of workers would be saved the stress of dealing with their computers crashing. So maybe more conservation policies for the workplace would be a good thing. The amount of work done by staff would be significantly reduced, but at least we'd all be protecting the planet. And who could disagree that that's only a small price to pay?

3 Non-fiction and media reading

Now answer this question:

- **What is the writer's attitude towards conservation? Remember to support your comments with evidence from the text.**

Write about one side of A4 paper 'against the clock' in about 15 minutes, as you would in an exam.

Exam tips

- Learn how to deal with the word **attitude** in a question. It requires some kind of cautious overall sense of what is going on and what the writer's (or character's) thoughts are. Attitudes can change quickly or slowly; attitudes can be very clear or very subtle.
- Use quotations freely, but do not drag out a quotation any longer than it need be. Sometimes a key word, sometimes a phrase, sometimes a whole sentence is needed (but judge it wisely). Use quotations as an aid to explaining, not as a substitute for it.
- Proper explanations sometimes require a little more of your time, an extra sentence. That extra sentence may clarify a point you wish to make and earn you an extra mark for your trouble.

Complete grids like those below before you write your full answer.

What means of persuasion does the brochure use? Does it threaten, warn, promise, tempt, flatter, encourage, bribe or challenge you? Choose two or three, including one of your own if you wish.

MEANS OF PERSUASION	COMMENT/EVIDENCE

What general qualities do the camp and its staff appear to advertise? Do they seem to be disciplined, friendly, cheap, hardworking, well-organized, available, overbearing, energetic, sophisticated, enthusiastic, reassuring, professional, authoritarian? Choose three or four of these (or add your own).

QUALITIES SUGGESTED	COMMENT/EVIDENCE

Which words and phrases in the text might be particularly worthy of comment?

WORDS AND PHRASES	COMMENT
'special rates for single parents'	
'the ultimate in luxury holiday accommodation'	
'well-trained staff'	

Read the following brochure material from Sunny Valley Holiday Camp. You will be answering the question: *How does the brochure try to persuade people to visit Sunny Valley Holiday Camp?* so focus on the text and identify relevant information that will support your comments.

Holiday fun in Sunny Valley

Sunny Valley is located on the Cornish coast and offers fun for people of all ages. Sunny Valley Holiday Camp has chalets, caravans and room for tents so it is suitable however you like to holiday. We welcome families and couples and even offer special rates for single parents to bring their children. Our chalets are spacious and comprise an attractive living area, two bedrooms and even a kitchen, with a microwave and fridge-freezer so you can stock up with all the Cornish specialities. For larger parties we recommend our six and eight berth caravans – the ultimate in luxury holiday accommodation. Both chalets and caravans have hot and cold water, power showers and the latest in satellite television entertainments. Everyone who holidays at Sunny Valley is assigned a Holiday Guide who will ensure they have the best time possible.

Parents need not worry about their children being bored. Here at Sunny Valley we have won numerous awards for our children's facilities. For the little ones (up to four years of age) there is a crèche and Junior Kids' Club. These offer mum and dad the chance to relax and spend some well-earned uninterrupted time together. Our well-trained staff have tons of activities prepared to ensure your children are never bored. For five to ten-year-olds there is the Big Kids Club that offers activities such as mini-golf, bowling, go-karting and a party each Friday afternoon. The children can also participate in art and craft classes and make their own fab souvenirs to remind them of their holiday at Sunny Valley. Teenagers are often hard to please, but here at Sunny Valley we offer the Teen Club, offering go-karting, abseiling, rock climbing and other challenges that would tempt even the most difficult teen. Each Friday night there is a disco for all Teen Club members to attend.

There are plenty of entertainments for adults too. If granny and granddad need a break, we have daily Bingo sessions, sing-along around our grand piano and tea dances three times a week. After all, at Sunny Valley we believe a holiday should please everyone, not just the children. For more adventurous adults, there are boat trips, steam engine journeys and even a chance to race go-karts like the kids!

Now answer the question:

* **How does the brochure try to persuade people to visit Sunny Valley Holiday Camp?**

You will notice that this article tries to persuade the reader in a way that is fairly typical of holiday camp brochures. Everyone seems welcome to visit, but surely the camp is designed for families and young people, though possibly not independent 18–30 groups. Needless to say perhaps, there are no art galleries or bookshops mentioned either. So beware using sweeping generalizations – Sunny Valley would not be to everyone's taste!

Complete grids like those below before you write your full answer.

What means of persuasion does the brochure use? Does it threaten, warn, promise, tempt, flatter, encourage, bribe or challenge you? Choose two or three, including one of your own if you wish.

MEANS OF PERSUASION	COMMENT/EVIDENCE

What general qualities do the camp and its staff appear to advertise? Do they seem to be disciplined, friendly, cheap, hardworking, well-organized, available, overbearing, energetic, sophisticated, enthusiastic, reassuring, professional, authoritarian? Choose three or four of these (or add your own).

QUALITIES SUGGESTED	COMMENT/EVIDENCE

Which words and phrases in the text might be particularly worthy of comment?

WORDS AND PHRASES	COMMENT
'special rates for single parents'	
'the ultimate in luxury holiday accommodation'	
'well-trained staff'	

Now answer this question:

* **What is the writer's attitude towards conservation? Remember to support your comments with evidence from the text.**

Write about one side of A4 paper 'against the clock' in about 15 minutes, as you would in an exam.

Exam tips

* Learn how to deal with the word **attitude** in a question. It requires some kind of cautious overall sense of what is going on and what the writer's (or character's) thoughts are. Attitudes can change quickly or slowly; attitudes can be very clear or very subtle.
* Use quotations freely, but do not drag out a quotation any longer than it need be. Sometimes a key word, sometimes a phrase, sometimes a whole sentence is needed (but judge it wisely). Use quotations as an aid to explaining, not as a substitute for it.
* Proper explanations sometimes require a little more of your time, an extra sentence. That extra sentence may clarify a point you wish to make and earn you an extra mark for your trouble.

Unit 3.3 Analysing persuasive techniques

What attitudes to ____ is the article trying to encourage? How does it try to encourage these attitudes?

How does the brochure try to persuade ____ ?

How does the article convey the horror of ____ ?

What image of the ____ is presented in the factsheet? How is this image created?

These questions focus on the point of view the writer is trying to get the audience to adopt. Analysing persuasive techniques means looking closely at the ways people try to 'sell' us something – often a product that we can buy in a shop, but just as likely an idea, an opinion, a way of seeing the world. Sometimes the writer may be opposed to something and may wish you to oppose it too; sometimes the writer may be in favour of something and may try to get you to agree.

The key to these questions is to focus on **how** the writer is persuading the audience. You need to consider what is written, how it is written and the intended effect of the words that have been chosen. There may be other features of the text as well as the language – a headline, pictures, inset boxes, for example.

Make sure you stay focused on the persuasive techniques adopted by the writer. Think of a range of tricks people play to persuade you – they may make you laugh to win you over, they may shock you into action, they may just quietly but insistently give you the facts. Be alert to all of the techniques that are available and collect them as you proceed through this unit. Make a mental note of persuasive techniques as you watch television (adverts particularly) and as you interact with and observe people in your daily life.

Emotive language (sometimes called 'loaded' language) is a key issue in persuasion. The connotations (the suggested meaning) of well-chosen, subtle words and phrases may have a persuasive impact on a reader.

Analysis of persuasive techniques, therefore, is partly a matter of content (**what** is said) and partly a matter of style (**how** it is said).

What might be worthy of comment about pictures and layout?

FEATURE OF PICTURE OR LAYOUT	COMMENT

Read 'Young Britons Quizzed Over State of the Planet' which is based on an article that appeared in the *Telegraph*. Consider what images of children are often in the news and how children are presented in this article.

Young Britons Quizzed Over State of the Planet

Young Britons are passionate about the future of the planet, with 80 per cent of 10- to 11-year-olds saying it is "very important" to look after the environment. Research carried out by NOP Family for Yellow Pages found 99 per cent of youngsters put their rubbish in the bin, 81 per cent recycle and 68 per cent walk to school.

The poll was commissioned to mark the launch of the Yellow Woods Challenge, a new schools recycling initiative run by Yellow Pages, the Directory Recycling Scheme and the Woodland Trust. Their biggest worries are about pollution from cars (47 per cent) and the dearth of rubbish facilities (32 per cent).

When it comes to questions about landfill and the ultimate destination of their rubbish, 41 per cent of boys realise it is taken to be buried in the ground, compared to only a third of girls.

And while almost one in five girls think that their dustbin's contents "just go away", only 13 per cent of boys think their rubbish simply disappears. Children are also very aware of the importance of trees to the environment. Some 86 per cent of those questioned knew that trees help the earth to breathe, 96 per cent understood that trees provide homes for wildlife, while 83 per cent saw trees as havens for animals and insects.

Michael Meacher, the Environment Minister, said: "The Yellow Woods Challenge is a fantastic example of how we can educate our children about the merit of recycling and the importance of our environment ... By working in partnership with local authorities and environmental organisations, Yellow Pages and the Directory Recycling Scheme will also be supporting the invaluable work of the Woodland Trust to protect the UK's woodland heritage."

Now answer the following question:

◆ **What image of young Britons is presented in this article? How is this image created?**

It is important to note that this question has two parts to it:

1   What image of young Britons is presented in this article?
2   How is this image created?

To answer this question properly you need to address both of these issues.

You may wish to use the following unfinished sentences as prompts in your answer. You can of course ignore them if you know what you want to write.

Young Britons are presented in the article as ....
This image is very different from ....

They are usually seen as .... , but this article says ....
This suggests that .... and ....

By.......................... the article creates the impression that ....

The image of young people as.......................... is (partly) created
by ....

The statistics, such as .... , help to support the claim that
....
The article, in focusing on the younger generation, might imply
that ....

The comment from the Government minister reveals that
.... and suggests that ....

When analysing persuasive techniques it is important that you explain **how** the passage persuades people. You must study the words and phrases used in the text and the choice of pictures. You also need to comment on the overall content of the passage and what the writer is persuading you to do or think. Does the writer use threats? Does the writer create positive or negative images in the passage? Does the writer describe a problem and then offer the solution? Does the writer want to change your beliefs about a certain issue or product?

THE BURNING ISSUE

Deforestation was the burning issue of the nineties, but since it has slipped from the news headlines, it also seems to have slipped from people's consciousness. This really does seem like a case of out of sight, out of mind and that actually will be the case for trees if deforestation continues at the rate it is at the moment. Despite the efforts of charities like Rainforest Concern, the public seems bored with this problem and instead focuses on whatever global disaster is stealing the headlines – the potential threat of war, most likely. With around 17 million hectares of forest being destroyed each year (an area larger than Great Britain and Ireland) the public should not be so complacent.

Deforestation causes all manner of problems, not just the obvious or well-publicised ones of loss of air quality or the extinction of a multitude of species. It is a well-cited fact that the equatorial rainforests are home to a huge variety of species of animals, birds, plants and insects that are not found anywhere else in the world. These are only the species that we are aware of. Some parts of the forest are so dense that there may be many more species that are as yet undiscovered.

Ironically, if deforestation continues these species will not remain undiscovered for long; they will be discovered and then made extinct almost straight away.

The forests are home to people as well as birds and animals. Some 350 million people worldwide rely on the forests for food, shelter and fuel. Many of these are tribes that have lived in the forests for centuries, or even millennia, and their knowledge of the forests is being lost almost as quickly as the trees themselves. These tribes-people are aware of natural remedies for many illnesses and ailments, which we in the so-called developed world could utilise. Deforestation causes many physical problems too. Soil erosion, watershed destabilisation and an imbalance in the global climate are all potential problems caused by deforestation.

So what can be done? Instead of using slash and burn methods of forestry, we should rely on sustainable forests made up of trees that grow and mature quickly and easily. Only if we do this, can we hope to preserve our forests – and our planet – for future generations.

Now answer the following question:

♣ **How does the writer try to persuade us that deforestation is a problem that needs to be dealt with urgently?**

The writer is evidently strongly opposed to deforestation, and so would be most of the readers. An answer that deals with the problems caused by deforestation, as explained in the article, will be quite successful. But a response that has its focus on the key word **urgently** would be even better. Make sure that you explore the ways that this writer tries to **persuade** us – warns, accuses, frightens, appeals to us …

REMEMBER Look closely at the language used by the writer. Pick out and comment on key phrases that create an effect.

Read the article on the opposite page about the London Marathon from the magazine *Marathon News*.

At the Heart of the World's Greatest Marathon

In 1996, Flora became the sponsor of the London Marathon creating a partnership which has proven to be one of the most successful in the history of British sporting events.

The Flora London Marathon is now recognised as the greatest city-centre marathon in the world; not only by the runners and media, but by the organisers of the other leading marathons worldwide. It boasts the largest number of entrants. It also has a very strong élite field, lining up current and past Olympic and world champions alongside world record holders. But, at the heart of the day can be found the 30,000+ amateur, club and fun runners who make London such a unique and memorable occasion.

Each year thousands of participants run to raise money for their favoured charities, many wearing weird, wonderful, and often cumbersome fancy-dress outfits, ensuring that their marathon is the ultimate, albeit intensely personal, challenge. It is estimated that since the first London Marathon was staged in 1981 over £150m has been raised for charity.

So why does the relationship continue to be such a phenomenal success?

The 2003 event will be Flora's eighth year as sponsor, and it is a partnership which has flourished due to a good fit between sponsor and event. Flora has been helping people to look after their health for over 30 years. The London Marathon is widely seen as the nation's favourite healthy event. Both Flora and the London Marathon are keen to ensure the event is inclusive, for anyone and everyone.

Central to Flora's communication over the last few years has been the importance of promoting heart health. The Flora London Marathon brings to life the healthy heart message to participants, spectators, family and friends alike; demonstrates the benefits of leading a healthy lifestyle and the importance of maintaining a healthy heart by combining sensible diet with exercise.

The London Marathon serves as an inspiration to us all. For those of you who have been armchair spectators in the past, why not take up the challenge and apply for the 2003 event? If you feel the Marathon distance is beyond you, use it as inspiration to create your own personal sporting or fitness challenge and take your first steps towards a longer, healthier and happier lifestyle.

Not only do we believe the Flora London Marathon is the greatest, but, judging from quotes and feedback from the 2002 race, so does everyone else!

BBC Grandstand commentary

"… you run out of things to say, just absolutely astounding … the Flora London Marathon is top of the tree. Others such as New York and Chicago have had claims to be the world's best marathon, but they can't come close to this."

Paula Radcliffe – 2002 women's champion

"I can already imagine the noise of the crowds in London on April 14th. That is when I will fulfil one of my childhood dreams and take part in the Flora London Marathon."

Simon Barnes – the Times Sports Columnist of The Year

"The need for adventure bites hard, but Cape Horn and Everest are incompatible with the mortgage, the marriage, the school run, a sensible CV and a nice sofa. Have no fear the London Marathon is there … the London Marathon is not Everest, but it is better than being cooped up and safer than finding the source of the Nile. This is not the real Ulysses, but it beats the hell out of stagnation."

Letter to The Times

"… the London Marathon gave us competition, endeavour, human achievement, world records and personal triumphs."

The Times

"London can pride itself on having created a world-class sporting event in the guise of the classic British street party."

Now answer the following question:

♣ **How does this article try to convince us that the London Marathon is the world's greatest marathon?**

Answer this question 'against the clock', as you would in an exam. Attempt to complete your response in around 15 minutes, writing up to, but no more than, a page of A4 (assuming your handwriting to be of average size).

Before you start to write, think about:
- **what** is said
- **how** it is said
- the use of headlines and layout.

3 Non-fiction and media reading

Unit 3.4 Comparing non-fiction and media texts

These texts present different ways of dealing with ▮▮▮▮. Which of these texts has more impact on you – and why?

Compare the ways the two texts tell you about ▮▮▮▮.

Both of these texts are concerned with ▮▮▮▮. In what ways are they similar and in what ways are they different?

Which do you think is more convincing: the article or the advertisement – and why?

Which aspects of these texts do you find effective in influencing your views on ▮▮▮▮?

The images of ▮▮▮▮ presented in these two texts are very different. In what ways are they different?

(You should refer closely to both texts in your answer.)

Comparison is a difficult skill. Comparison tasks always present an organizational headache! The most important point to make in this brief introduction is that the question or task will not always be the same. You will, though, always be required to refer to two texts, not one. Sometimes you will be expected to make a direct comparison, while at other times you will be asked to decide which of two texts is more successful, and, as the sample questions above show, there are other styles of question too.

In this unit, two 'full length' pairs of texts are provided and there are alternative questions asked about each pair, so that you can be on alert for different perspectives. As a bonus, a shorter pair of texts appears in the middle of the unit to allow for specific practice on comparing details of language.

Grids seem particularly useful in this unit because of the importance of clear organization, but please note that you should not present your final answer in the exam in grid form. Grids cannot cope with subtle explanations of comparison, so they have their limitations – they are useful for teaching the importance of organization and structure.

Non-fiction and media are two closely linked categories of text. Reports, articles, advertisements, autobiographies and other types of text could be represented, with the Internet probably playing an increasing role, as in this unit. Leaflets, for example, now appear freely on the Internet, but, in doing so, change their form. The purpose and audience of a text are generally more important than the genre (the label that may be put on a text).

In all, the comparison question tests knowledge and use of text, particularly cross-referencing, but it also involves inference and interpretation, appreciation and evaluation of language, structure and presentational features. You should explore both texts, though a perfect balance in your coverage of the two is not expected.

Read this report by Bob Thomas from an American newspaper, the *Houston Chronicle*, about the 30th anniversary of the last moon landing.

Passage 1

Astronauts Mark 30th Anniversary of Last Moon Landing

Beverly Hills, California – Thirty years have passed, but no amount of time could dim the vivid memory Eugene Cernan has of being the last person to leave footprints on the moon.

"It's like you would want to freeze that moment and take it home with you. But you can't," Cernan recalled as he joined fellow Apollo 17 astronaut Harrison Schmitt and other aviation pioneers to celebrate the 30th anniversary of the last manned mission to the moon.

As he made his way up the ladder to his spacecraft for the trip back to Earth, Cernan struggled for words to leave behind. He said he realised they wouldn't be as memorable as Neil Armstrong's comment when he became the first person to set foot on the moon: "That's one small step for a man, one giant leap for mankind."

Cernan's parting remark: "We now leave as we once came, and God willing we shall return with peace and hope for all mankind."

Cernan said at Friday's gathering it never occurred to him that 30 years later he'd still be the last man on the moon.

"We knew Apollo 17 was going to be the final [Apollo] flight," he said. "And I knew that I would take the last steps on the moon. But never in my wildest dreams did I imagine that it would be the last time for a generation or so."

Other astronauts at the Friday night dinner at the estate of entrepreneur and space enthusiast Robert H. Lorsch included Edwin "Buzz" Aldrin of Apollo

11, T.R. Mattingly of Apollo 16, and James Lovell of Apollo 13.

The dinner was a benefit for the Astronaut Scholarship Foundation, which supports advanced education for college students of science and technology. Mainly, it gave the astronauts a chance to share memories of the most exciting time of their lives.

The 1970 voyage of Apollo 13, which Lovell commanded, also was to have included a moon landing, but it had to be aborted after an oxygen tank ruptured aboard the moon-bound spacecraft. Lovell was portrayed by Tom Hanks in the movie *Apollo 13*, about the near-fatal mission.

Lovell noted that Apollo 18 and 19 were also planned as moon missions but that NASA cancelled them, perhaps because of his mission's near-disaster. "I think [cancelling] was a grave mistake," he said Friday night. "We had only touched a couple of places [on the moon]; there were other places we could have gone to. The scientific community was very dissatisfied."

Cernan hopes to see that situation corrected. "I came back from the mission and got on my soapbox," he said. "The press continued to ask me, 'How does it feel to be the tail of the dog, the last one over the fence.' I said, 'Apollo 17 is not the end; it's the beginning of a whole new era in the history of mankind. Not only will we go to the moon, but we'll be on our way to Mars by the turn of the century.'"

3 Non-fiction and media reading

Now read the following advertisement (in the form of an article) for a video. It is from a website, Aulis Online. Aulis publishes works that oppose established thought. Its aim is to present alternative ideas and to stimulate fresh thinking – and to sell videos ...

What Happened on the Moon? An Investigation into Apollo

The majority of us believe we went to the Moon in 1969 – it represents a tremendous achievement for mankind, the first time we have landed and walked upon another celestial body.

But what really happened on the Moon in 1969?

Five years in the making, *What Happened on the Moon? An Investigation into Apollo*, is now available in a two-tape video set.

This compelling video throws into serious doubt the authenticity of the Apollo missions and features information that challenges the declared abilities of NASA to successfully send a man to the Moon and return him safely to Earth.

"If some of the film was spoiled, it's remotely possible they [NASA] may have shot some scenes in a studio environment to avoid embarrassment."

Dr Brian O'Leary, astronaut

Did the Apollo missions really achieve NASA's aims? This enthralling production presents the flaws in the record of this landmark event in a graphic, dynamic, easy-to-follow way.

What Happened on the Moon? examines the problems with rockets and associated technologies as well as the serious dangers – that to date have not been overcome – concerning deep space radiation. Why was faking necessary? Hear what NASA has to say in response to these disturbing findings.

"Of all history's great conspiracy theories – one of the most enduring, and one with which I have particular sympathy, is concerned with men landing on the Moon. Was it all, as some have reasonably opined, not a lunar touchdown but instead a strikingly recreated stunt on a movie sound stage ... well away from prying eyes?"

Quentin Falk, The *Daily Telegraph*. From a review of *Capricorn One*

New evidence revealing significant errors in continuity between the Apollo still photos and the 'live' TV coverage suggests that NASA hoaxed the official record of mankind's first visit to the Moon.

These new findings are supported by detailed analysis and the testimony of experts from various disciplines. These include photographer/filmmaker David S Percy ARPS and physicist David Groves PhD. The numerous inconsistencies visible in the images are quite irrefutable.

Recent research indicates that the errors evidenced were deliberately planted by individuals determined to leave clues pointing to the faking of the record of Apollo.

The main thrust of this video is to question the entire validity of the official record of mankind's exploration of the Moon. Sending men to the Moon and bringing them back safely is widely held to be the greatest technical achievement of mankind so far. In fact the greatest achievement of the second millennium. Indeed the landing of the Apollo astronauts on the Moon is now considered by many to be the benchmark by which human endeavour is measured.

A benchmark which might well be invalid.

***What Happened on the Moon?* The video will reveal all.**

Now answer the following question:

♦ **Which of these two texts, the report or the article, do you find more interesting – and why?**

There is no right answer to this question – you can choose either of these texts as the more interesting one. However, you should bring both texts into your discussion. Therefore, you should make comments about the text that you find less interesting (or, indeed, not interesting at all).

Answers to comparative questions are sometimes too long – often (though not always) it is the last question in the section of the exam and therefore the last chance to offload anything you can think of. Don't fall for this – compile a handful of points (four or five) that you can state clearly, some of them making direct links between the two texts.

Use a grid like the one below to jot down some clear points in note form, developing them if you can on occasions to include direct comparisons. Your final response should read fluently, so try to avoid using the same sentence opening each time.

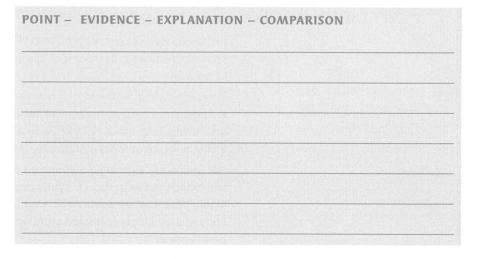

POINT – EVIDENCE – EXPLANATION – COMPARISON

Alternative task

You may wish to tackle a different comparative question for these two texts to enable you to practise on the focus of different styles of question:

♦ **Both of these texts are concerned with the American moon landings. In what ways are they similar and in what ways are they different.**

Here is a possible opening of an answer to the above question:
Both of these passages are about landing on the moon. The first passage celebrates the fact that it is the anniversary of the last moon landing. The article is congratulating NASA and Mankind in general for its achievement. The tone of the passage is positive and almost gives the impression that humans can do anything! The second passage is an advertisement for a video that claims to contain evidence that the moon landing was a hoax and that we have not really landed on the moon ...

3 Non-fiction and media reading

Either continue the above answer or write a complete answer of your own. Use grids like the ones below to help you to compile your points.

SIMILARITIES (i.e. close comparisons, but not necessarily identical features)

REPORT (*Houston Chronicle*)	ARTICLE/ADVERT (Aulis Online)

DIFFERENCES (moving towards contrasts or opposites)

REPORT (*Houston Chronicle*)	ARTICLE/ADVERT (Aulis Online)

A language study

Read these two short texts about water. The first advertises Brecon Carreg bottled water, the second is the beginning of an encyclopedia entry from *The Hutchinson Softback Encyclopedia.*

Wild Welsh Water

Wild Water from Wales?

Brecon Carreg is wild in every sense. Conceived far out in the Atlantic, delivered by the west winds onto the Black Mountain deep within the Brecon Beacons National Park. Where for 15 years it percolates through the limestone strata, being naturally purified and gaining its unique fresh taste.

It emerges at the source, protected by nature and us, to be bottled as 'Natural Mineral Water'.

Brecon Carreg is the most popular Welsh water in Wales, safely fuelling the national passion for sport, music, culture and life itself – there's nothing tame about the Welsh or Brecon Carreg!

BRECON CARREG

NATURAL MINERAL WATER

Water (H_2O) a liquid without colour, taste, or odour. It is an oxide of hydrogen. Water begins to freeze solid at 0°C or 32°F, and to boil at 100°C or 212°F. When liquid, it is virtually incompressible; frozen, it expands by 1/11 of its volume. 1 cubic cm weighs 1 gram at 4°C, its maximum density, forming the unit of specific gravity. It has the highest known specific heat, and acts as an efficient solvent, particularly when hot. Most of the world's water is in the sea; less than 0.01% is fresh water.

Water takes the form of sea, rain, and vapour, and supports all forms of land and marine life. As distinct from heavy water, which contains deuterium, ordinary water is sometimes referred to as 'light water'.

The texts on page 95 would be too short for inclusion in the examination, but here they provide an excellent opportunity to focus on certain features of non-fiction and media writing, particularly the **purpose** of each text (why each one was written) and the **details of language** in each text.

They also provide an opportunity to practise responding to the most conventional comparative task:

Compare the advertisement and the encyclopedia entry.

You should consider:

– the purpose of each text

– the content of each text

– the image of water in each text

– the choice of language in each text

– the overall presentation of each text.

In a task like this, you really should take advantage of the points listed. Practise by compiling them thoroughly in grid form:

POINTS TO CONSIDER	DETAILS AND/OR COMMENTS
The purpose of each text	
The content of each text	
The image of water in each text	
The choice of language in each text	
The overall presentation of each text	

NOTE The choice of language could include words and phrases, also sentence styles.

Now write an organized and fluent response to the task:

⬥ **Compare the advertisement and the encyclopedia entry.**

Read the following articles.

The first is by Nigel Williamson from the *Times Educational Supplement*, in which pop star Mick Jagger talks about his school days at Dartford Grammar School. He has recently had an arts block at the school named after him, about forty years after leaving.

The second is taken from the website of the Teacher Training Agency, which is responsible for recruiting new teachers into the profession.

At the end you will be asked to respond to the question: *'Which aspects of these texts do you find effective in influencing your views on teaching?'* so bear this in mind as you read.

3 Non-fiction and media reading

MICK JAGGER, POP STAR – MY BEST TEACHER

by Nigel Williamson

I've been back to Dartford over the years, but I hadn't been back to the grammar school until now. It's a strange feeling, because you want to be on your best behaviour. When you walk through the gates you remember that's where you got in a fight or that's where you got busted for not wearing the correct uniform. But I was a good, rounded person because I wasn't a swot and I wasn't a dunce. I was in the middle ground.

There was real violence between masters and pupils. There were guerrilla skirmishes on all fronts, with civil disobedience and undeclared war; they threw blackboard rubbers at us and we threw them back.

There were paper darts, pea-shooters, catapults. It was like something out of a cartoon in a comic book – *The Beano*, or something.

We used to get caned. It was routine everyday, with a line of boys standing outside the head's study. He was called "Lofty" Herman and he was a classic short person. He had very disciplined ideas and strange notions about social life. I didn't like him at all. I don't think anybody did.

He was an iron-fisted disciplinarian: totally cold and unapproachable. You had to wait outside the study until the light went on and then you'd go in. And everybody else used to hang about on the stairs to see how many he gave and how bad it was that morning.

Every master had his own tortures. There were some who would just punch you out. They'd slap your face so hard you'd go down. Others would twist your ear and drag you along until it was red and stinging. It was another world. They wouldn't get away with it today.

It's such a cliché that your school days are the happiest of your life. It really wasn't very pleasant. There was far too much petty discipline. There were incredibly petty rules about uniforms. There was a girls' grammar school across the street, and you weren't even allowed to speak to them at the bus stop.

It was hard work. If you had other interests like singing or dancing you seemed to have very few hours for them. The weekend was taken up with homework. I remember getting up at 6am to finish my homework because I'd fallen asleep over it the previous night, especially during the second year of A-levels.

Some of the masters were better than others. Arthur Page, the sports master, he was okay. He was a friend of my father, Joe, who also taught sports as well as history at other Dartford schools. Having a teacher as a parent meant you couldn't lie about your homework, but at least they could help you with it. They would know the syllabus and the cribs for your Latin and how to pass the exam.

I did Latin for five years, but today I couldn't translate a three-word Latin tag. We used to rag the Latin master something terrible because he never really punished anyone. We used to throw the rubber dusters at the blackboard while he was writing on it. Then he'd turn round and you'd be yellow carded. Keeping order was really a problem. It was all streamed and our class was one of the better ones so I hate to think what the less interested groups were like.

There was one really good maths guy who wasn't actually my teacher. But he was another friend of my father's and he helped get me through my maths because I found that tricky. My history master, Walter Wilkinson, was good, despite the fact he had a really imperialist view of history. We used to throw football boots at the English master, just to keep ourselves amused and relieve the boredom of English poetry appreciation. Sweet Mr Brandon. He didn't deserve the ragging we gave him. He was such a gentle man.

We didn't make their lives any easier. It was terrible what we did, really. Even the ones who were okay got caught in the crossfire. The behaviour patterns were entrenched; we abused them whether they were decent or not. I was famous for mimicking them. You spent so long watching them, you could get them down to a fine art.

I read in the prospectus that the emphasis is now on self-discipline rather than corporal punishment, which is wonderful. The whole climate today is different. I think attitudes changed when they stopped using so much corporal punishment. It wasn't just the caning; there was a whole culture of violence. It was fear and loathing in north Kent. A different way of teaching came in during the Sixties which probably in some places has gone too far in the other direction.

Now the school has got this new performing arts centre, which is wonderful. There are so many different things they can do there: music, theatre, films, video. When I was at the school you got the feeling that arts and music were very much on the edge of the syllabus. I started a record club and we'd sit there in the lunch hour with a master behind the desk frowning while we played Lonnie Donegan records. That's all we had. If we had a facility like this new centre it would have made a fantastic difference. It would have gathered together all the people who had been in the closet, because it was a bit like being in the closet wanting to be a musician in those days. Nobody wanted to admit it. It wasn't a serious job like being the assistant manager of a bank.

Some of the masters rather begrudgingly enjoyed music, but they couldn't own up to it. There was a general feeling that music wasn't important. But we had the stereotypical modern master who liked trad jazz. Dave Brubeck was very popular. It was cool to like that and it wasn't cool to like rock 'n' roll. Jazz was intelligent and people with glasses played it, so we all had to make out we liked Gerry Mulligan. ∎

Are **you** inspired by the idea of pursuing a career in which you make a genuine difference to people's lives? Do you want to play an active role in your community? Are you excited by the prospect of helping young people to develop knowledge, and learn new skills? Teachers are driven by these opportunities, and committed to providing the best education to the children and young people they teach.

What is teaching like?

▶ It's fulfilling. After all, you'll be educating and shaping the development of a new generation. Imagine the satisfaction of helping young people turn their ambitions into reality.

▶ It's life changing. In teaching someone to read, do sums, learn a new language or understand the laws of science, you will be equipping them for life. Giving young people the opportunity to develop, to enable them to fulfil their aspirations and then exceed them will not only be rewarding for you, it will mean the world to others. You will give your pupils the opportunity to lead informed and successful lives.

▶ It's hard work. Teaching requires the highest level of commitment, to pupils and colleagues. Outside the classroom teachers are expected to prepare lessons, mark their pupils' work and contribute to the running of the school, through meeting with and supporting the other staff. Many teachers take on responsibilities outside the classroom, be it on the sports field or supervising school outings.

▶ It's fun. People often forget how much fun working with children and young adults can be. Remember how hilarious school plays and trips were? How many careers offer the chance to share in the enthusiasm and excitement of young people? You will relish tackling new challenges, and reaping the rewards, every day.

Teaching offers a range of opportunities and benefits that are the envy of other professions the world over. Boredom is not on the syllabus.

Now answer the following question:
◆ **Which aspects of these texts do you find effective in influencing your views on teaching?**

Answer this question 'against the clock', as you would in an exam. Write between half a side and a full side of A4 paper in no more than 15 minutes.

In this task you should pick out and comment on the words and phrases, the images and the ideas from both texts that have made some impact on you. Your views on teaching may be well formed (or not), but you should treat the texts with objective interest. The question does not assume that you do (or did!) want to become a teacher. It perhaps does assume that you will have some understanding of teaching styles and educational issues. There is an element of personal response in the question, but the key focus is the texts.

Now consider this alternative question on the same texts:

🔸 **The images of teaching presented in these texts are very different. In what ways are they different?**

Again, Try to write your response (between half a side and a full side of A4 paper) in no more than 15 minutes.

This question is slanted differently from the earlier one. Here you are expected to look at sharp differences between, if you like, the idealized teacher of the future and the hatchet man of the past! In the Mick Jagger piece, it is not all doom and gloom, but the question does require you to focus mainly on **the difference of image**.

Exam tips

🔸 Answer the question that you have been asked, not the one you would have liked to be asked!

🔸 Make sure that you refer to both texts.

🔸 If you are given a list of points to consider, do it. But don't expect to find an equal number of comments to make about each point.

🔸 Organize and control your answer. Do not go rambling on and on.

🔸 Avoid simple assertions based on vague 'media' drill, e.g. 'I prefer the first text because it has a picture … The other one is boring because it uses big words …'

🔸 Don't answer in grid form in the exam. Grids are useful for sorting out your material, but they cannot do the explaining!

Transactional and discursive writing

Section B (Writing:15%) will test **transactional** and **discursive** writing through two equally weighted tasks, the first of which will be linked to the reading material in Section A (non-fiction and media). The first will ask for a piece of writing intended to *argue, persuade, advise*. The second will offer opportunities to *analyse, review, comment*.

In transactional writing tasks, the writer generally has a clear point or points to make to the reader(s) or listener(s). There are several forms of transactional writing which are covered by writing to *argue, persuade, advise*. These include formal letters, leaflets and factsheets, reports and speeches.

In discursive writing, too, the writer will generally have a clear point of view to put across to the reader(s). Articles and reviews are popular forms of discursive writing, as covered by writing to *analyse, review, comment*. (Note that formal letters, etc. might also qualify as discursive writing in many cases.)

When your examination writing is marked, it will be assessed in terms of:
a content and organization
b sentence structure, punctuation and spelling.

This section of the book contains three units:

4.1 Writing to *argue, persuade, advise* You will learn about the content and organization of formal letter, leaflet and factsheet, report and speech writing.

4.2 Writing to *analyse, review, comment* You will learn about the content and organization of article and review writing.

4.3 Technical accuracy in transactional and discursive writing You will examine sentence structure, punctuation and spelling in relation to transactional and discursive writing.

Writing to argue, persuade, advise

Transactional writing

When writing to **argue**, **persuade** or **advise** you will probably write with knowledge of the particular topic or issue concerned. You may have strong opinions to *argue* and sound *advice* to give. You may be capable of *persuading* someone to change to your point of view. Writing with these purposes in mind can take many forms: formal letters, leaflets and factsheets, reports, speeches.

When writing documents like these, consider the:
- purpose – why you are writing
- audience – who you are writing for
- format – how you organize the layout of the writing.

Formal letters

Formal letters require a particular layout and style of writing. These are important points to remember when completing a letter task.

The key to writing formal letters is to put forward your point persuasively and convince the person receiving your letter to adopt the same opinion as you.

You can use 'I' and 'me' in letters because you are addressing directly the person you are writing to. However, you must still keep your tone reasonably formal and polite.

> *Here are some examples of the sorts of letter that you might be asked to write in the exam:*
>
> Write a letter to your MP. You may argue for or against fox hunting.
>
> A newspaper has recently printed an article arguing that movie stars are paid too much money. Write a letter to the newspaper giving your views on this issue.
>
> Write a letter to your head teacher with your recommendations for improving your school uniform.
>
> A local hotel/restaurant is advertising for part-time staff. Write a letter of application.

To start your letter, remember to write your address (or the address of the school or college, if you prefer) in the top right-hand corner. Then write the date underneath this. Underneath your address and the date, and on the left-hand side of the page, write the name and address of the person to whom you are writing. This will usually be given to you in the examination. Address your letter 'Dear Sir or Madam' if you do not know the name of the person you are writing to or, for example, 'Dear Mr Jones' if you do.

Read the following in response to: *'Write a letter to your MP. You may argue for or against fox hunting.'* (A few tips have been included to help you.)

19 Chapel Road
Anytown
AN1 10W

27 May 2003

Robin Parker MP
Houses of Parliament
Westminster
London W1

Dear Mr Parker

You could begin your letter by introducing yourself briefly and explaining why you are writing about this topic. Make your argument clear from the opening paragraph. This will immediately grab the attention of your reader and make them take notice of what you are arguing for.

When the task does not give you a clear point of view to argue in your letter, you must adopt one of your own. This will be either in favour of or against the issue. In this particular task, a point of view has not been given, so the writer must decide whether they are in favour of fox hunting or against it. For example:

I am a student at Holly Community College in Anytown. Anytown is a rural community and we are surrounded by lots of small farms and open fields. The farmers rely on their livestock for their income and at the moment their livestock is being threatened by an increasing population of foxes. I urge you to stop fox hunting from being banned, to prevent the farmers' livelihood from being destroyed. My father is a farmer and I can see the damage that foxes cause to our stock.

It is also possible to write an opening paragraph that adopts the opposite point of view:

I am a student at Holly Community College in Anytown. Anytown is a rural community and we are surrounded by lots of small farms and open fields. Our school is set on the edge of one of these fields and we encourage the local wildlife as much as possible. Recently, however, there has been a significant decrease in the numbers of foxes that have been seen around the school. This can only be because of the fox hunting that takes place regularly in this area. Fox hunting is cruel and unnecessary and I urge you to make sure a law is passed banning it. I do not think it has any benefits to our local area. The farmers complain that the foxes kill one or two of their chickens, but if they were caged in properly this would not happen.

Now complete the following task:

* **Write the opening paragraph for a response to the task: 'Write a letter to your MP. You may argue for or against the use of animals in experiments.'**

Remember to lay out the addresses and the date properly.

Here is another example where the writer has to decide which point of view to adopt: '*A newspaper has recently printed an article arguing that celebrities are paid too much money. Write a letter to the newspaper giving your views on this issue.*'

The tasks given in the exam are likely to involve quite controversial subjects where you will have a point of view, one way or the other.

Dear Editor,

After reading your recent article about the current wages of stars in sport and entertainment, I felt I had to write a letter in response. I think that movie stars, for instance, deserve the money they earn. Movie making is a demanding and competitive business and movie stars are expected to work long hours in order to get the scene right. I also think that movie stars will only have short careers. Once they become older they are less attractive and less likely to get parts in films. I think they deserve their high wages as a compensation for having a short career. If they cannot get roles in films then they cannot work at all. I also think that movie stars need a lot of money to make up for the way they are treated by the newspapers. The newspapers print revealing photographs of them and write stories about them to sell newspapers. I think their high wages are a form of compensation for this too.

In this letter, the writer has adopted the view that celebrities (in this case, movie stars) are not paid too much and that they deserve the millions of pounds they receive.

Now complete the same task:

* **Write the opening paragraph for: 'A newspaper has recently printed an article arguing that movie stars are paid too much money. Write a letter to the newspaper giving your views on this issue.'**

However, argue the opposite point of view to the one presented above. Argue the case that celebrities do get paid too much. Remember to lay out the addresses and the date properly.

4 Transactional and discursive writing

After developing your argument, you need to finish your letter. You must write a conclusion that contains a final plea to the person to whom you are writing to adopt your point of view. Start by summarizing what you have written.

Read the following concluding paragraph in response to: *'Write a letter to your head teacher with your recommendations for improving your school uniform.'*

To conclude, although the school uniform is very practical, I do think it could be modified to make it more appealing for the students who have to wear it. On the whole, the school uniform is good but, by making the small changes I have suggested, the pupils would be much happier with it than they are currently. I am sure you will agree that if the school insists on its pupils wearing school uniform, it is only fair that they have some say in the way it looks.

Now complete the following task:
- **Write the closing paragraph for: 'Write a letter to your head teacher or principal with your recommendations for improving the appearance of the school or college.'**

Conventions of formal letter writing

It is fair to say that the rules (or conventions) of formal letter writing are less strict these days than they were before the age of computers.

Addresses and date
- Make sure that your address, as the writer of the letter, is on the top right of the letter.
- The date on which the letter is being written should be underneath the writer's address.
- If you write a formal letter, to anyone in an organization, remember to put their name and address details on the left, above the body of the letter.
- Traditionally, commas were expected at the end of each line of an address, but the rule has been relaxed. However, be consistent one way or the other – commas or no commas, not a mixture of the two.

Dear_____ and Yours_____
- For letters that start with 'Dear Sir or Madam', end with 'Yours faithfully'.
- For letters that start with, for example, 'Dear Mr Jones', end with 'Yours sincerely'.
- In reality, however, there are plenty of circumstances when the decision rests with the writer. The point that remains true is that *Yours faithfully* is more formal than *Yours sincerely*.

Now complete the following tasks:

- **Consider everything that has been covered in this unit and then write a letter to your local newspaper on the subject: 'The government has decided to crack down on anti-social behaviour, which might mean anything from dropping chewing gum on the pavement to drunken behaviour in public. Discuss anti-social behaviour in your area and how it might be tackled.'**

- **Return to your group list of topics and issues and choose the one about which you feel most strongly. Write a letter to a newspaper raising and discussing your issue of topical interest. Try to focus on a particular argument that could win people over to your point of view.**

Write your letter 'against the clock' in about 30 minutes.

REMEMBER When writing to a newspaper, you would normally write to the editor **but** this is for the general public to read, it is not a private letter.

Leaflets and factsheets

Leaflets and factsheets require precise and specific information. This has to be presented in a way that is easy to understand.

> Here are some examples of the sorts of task that you might be asked to complete in your exam:
>
> Write a leaflet for parents offering advice about recycling in the home.
>
> Write a leaflet for teenagers offering advice for giving up smoking.
>
> Write a factsheet for younger students highlighting the dangers of taking drugs.

There is very little practical difference between a leaflet and a factsheet, as confirmed by these dictionary definitions:

Leaflet – A sheet of (usually printed) paper (sometimes folded but not stitched) giving information, especially for free distribution.

Factsheet – A paper setting out relevant information.

A leaflet might unofficially be expected to contain more opinions than facts, while the name factsheet suggests facts alone, without any opinions. In practice, factsheets do more than simply give facts in most cases. The term **leaflet** will be used for the rest of this section.

- Leaflets use clearly marked sub-sections with sub-headings, so that the reader can digest a large amount of information very easily.
- They are expected to be written in standard English.
- Often, a key feature of this type of writing is that the reader is addressed directly as 'you'.

The key to writing leaflets is to stay focused on the issue you are writing about. When starting your leaflet, you need to introduce the topic being discussed. This usually means using a heading to attract the reader's attention and then giving some explanation of what will be covered in the leaflet.

Read the following opening paragraph in response to: *'Write a leaflet for parents offering advice about recycling in the home.'*

RECYCLING IN THE HOME

Most of the waste produced by families could be recycled. Rubbish such as paper, cardboard, tins, cans and bottles can now be recycled, as well as all different types of plastic. If everybody began recycling we could reduce our total rubbish by over 50%. Recycling is not difficult and it can be incorporated easily into everyday life. It is something that everyone can do – even you!

In this leaflet, the writer has clearly introduced the topic and addresses the reader directly.

Now complete the following task:
- **Write the introductory paragraph for: 'Write a leaflet for elderly people offering advice about safety in the home.'**

After introducing the topic, it is a good idea to divide your leaflet into sub-sections, with sub-headings. This will make it easier for your reader to follow and understand the text. The sub-headings should be clearly related to the issue you are discussing. For the leaflet about recycling in the home, the sub-headings could be:
– What can be recycled?
– Reusing and recycling
– Where do I take my recycling to be processed?
– What are the consequences of not recycling?
– What are the benefits of recycling?

Now complete the following task:

🔹 **Devise five or six sub-headings for your leaflet about safety in the home.**

Each sub-heading should be followed by at least one paragraph of relevant text, written in standard English. Try to expand this sub-section as much as possible. For example:

WHAT CAN BE RECYCLED?

Almost everything that is classed as rubbish can be recycled. This includes paper, cardboard, clothes and even kitchen waste and scraps of food. There are certain types of plastic that cannot be recycled, but apart from this everything can either be reused or recycled.

Kitchen waste can be used as compost for the garden. This could be vegetable peelings, scraps of food or egg shells. All of this will break down and feed your garden. Remember also that, especially during winter, birds struggle to find food. Kitchen scraps could be used to feed them at this time of year. Birds will eat most kitchen waste, not just breadcrumbs!

Old clothes can be used as dusters, rags or bedding for pets. Good quality used clothes can be sent to charity shops and sold on to people who can make use of them.

The writer could now go on to complete the other sub-sections, following the structure of sub-headings listed above.

Now complete the following task:

🔹 **Select one or two of your sub-headings about safety in the home and write a relevant piece of text to go underneath.**

Read the following summarizing paragraph of a leaflet written in response to: *'Write a leaflet for teenagers offering advice for giving up smoking.'*

Final Word

There are plenty of ways to give up smoking. Do not be afraid to ask for help from family and friends or even local organisations, such as ASH, which specifically deal with issues related to smoking. The most important thing is not to give up giving up. Millions of people have been successful and you could soon be one of them.

Now complete the following task:

🔹 **End your leaflet about safety in the home by summarizing the contents. This again should be about one paragraph in length.**

4 Transactional and discursive writing

Conventions of leaflets and factsheets

♠ Leaflets have headings and sub-headings, which can be created in a draft form under pressure of time (as in the examination).

♠ Leaflets also often have pictures. The convention in a draft leaflet (i.e. in an examination) is an empty box or space quickly drawn in the appropriate part of the leaflet. It can be useful to write a caption for the imaginary picture.

♠ Bullet points are nowadays a common feature of leaflets. Use these in your leaflet, but do not overdo them.

♠ The written text of leaflets is often presented in columns. This is possible in a leaflet written in an examination, but not necessary.

♠ Leaflets are generally folded pieces of paper. However, you are not expected to fold your examination answer!

Now complete the following:

♠ **Consider everything that has been covered in this section and complete the task: 'Write a leaflet warning younger pupils about the dangers of fireworks.'**

♠ **Return to the group list of topics that you made at the start of the unit. Write a leaflet for adults on a topic of your choice, informing them what it is about and attempting to persuade them to your point of view.**

Write your leaflet 'against the clock' in about 30 minutes.

NOTE You may choose a fresh topic if you wish OR you may repeat your coverage of the topic that you chose for letter-writing. If you do the latter, make sure that your material now fits the leaflet format effectively.

Reports

Reports are in some ways more formal versions of leaflets. They introduce an issue and then suggest different ways of dealing with that issue.

> *Below are some possible reports that you might be asked to write in the exam:*
>
> The governors of your school would like the views of students about improving the appearance of the school. Write a report for the governors detailing these views.
>
> Write a report for your local council outlining ways in which the area surrounding your home could be improved.
>
> Your school is holding a charity event. Write a report for your head teacher outlining worthwhile charities that should benefit from your fund-raising.
>
> Write a report for an American company that is thinking about opening a factory in the UK. Outline the facilities available in your area that would make it appealing as a location for the factory.

The key to writing a good focused report is to use a clear title that indicates the topic of the report and to whom it is directed. This information is usually given in the task. Good reports also make use of sub-headings that focus the attention of the reader on specific aspects of the overall issue. Reports must be written in standard English and, unlike leaflets and factsheets, should not address the reader directly.

Once you have written a suitable title, you then need to give an overall explanation of the contents of the report.

Read the following title and introduction in response to: *'The governors of your school would like the views of students about improving the appearance of the school. Write a report for the governors detailing these views.'*

**REPORT FOR THE SCHOOL GOVERNORS ON
IMPROVING THE APPEARANCE OF THE SCHOOL**

From: Student council

To: Chair of governing body

INTRODUCTION

Most of the classrooms have recently been renovated to make them more modern and more comfortable for both teachers and students. However, the outside of the school building and the school grounds need attention to make them more appealing to everyone working at and attending the school. There are several areas that need specific attention. These are the exterior walls of the school building, the sports field, the playground, the netball court, the staff car park, and the courtyard at the front of the school.

The title of this report is taken from the task itself, which enables the writer to focus clearly on the requirements of the task. The introduction then details the specific areas of the school covered in the remainder of the report.

Now complete the following:
- **Write the title and introduction for the task: 'Write a report for your local council outlining ways in which the area surrounding your home could be improved.'**

The introduction to the report about the appearance of the school suggests six areas of the school that require attention. These would form natural sub-headings and are the:

- exterior walls of the school building
- sports field
- playground
- netball court
- staff car park
- courtyard at the front of the school.

Now complete the following task:
- **Devise five or six sub-headings for your report about the area surrounding your home.**

Under each sub-heading you should give an explanation of, for example, how this item or issue could be improved. Each of these should be at least one paragraph in length and must be written in standard English. Try to expand each sub-heading as much as possible. For example:

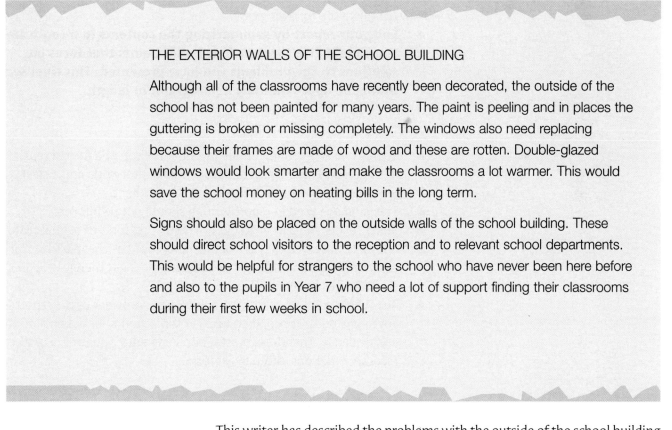

THE EXTERIOR WALLS OF THE SCHOOL BUILDING

Although all of the classrooms have recently been decorated, the outside of the school has not been painted for many years. The paint is peeling and in places the guttering is broken or missing completely. The windows also need replacing because their frames are made of wood and these are rotten. Double-glazed windows would look smarter and make the classrooms a lot warmer. This would save the school money on heating bills in the long term.

Signs should also be placed on the outside walls of the school building. These should direct school visitors to the reception and to relevant school departments. This would be helpful for strangers to the school who have never been here before and also to the pupils in Year 7 who need a lot of support finding their classrooms during their first few weeks in school.

This writer has described the problems with the outside of the school building and has even offered possible solutions to some of them. They would then go on to expand upon each of the other sub-headings in the report.

Now complete the following task:
- **Select one or two of your sub-headings and write a relevant piece of text to go underneath.**

Read the following summarizing paragraph of a report written in response to: *'Your school is holding a charity event. Write a report for your head teacher outlining worthwhile charities that should benefit from your fund-raising.'*

CONCLUSION

Although there are many worthwhile charities in our local area, there are only three or four that would be relevant to the students of our school. These are:

❑ The RSPCA – most students love animals and have pets of their own. Many students would support the idea of raising money for this charity.

❑ The NSPCC – this charity works with children and the students would like to help their peers who are less fortunate than themselves.

❑ The NCH – this charity also works with children and the students would want to help children who do not have stable families.

❑ Childline – this charity offers support to children who have no one else to turn to when they are being bullied or abused.

Now complete the following task:

♣ **End your report by summarizing the contents in a conclusion. You should give three or four bullet points that focus on solutions to the problems you have presented. This final section should be approximately a paragraph in length.**

Conventions of report writing

♣ There is no strict ruling on the layout at the top of a formal report, but it is necessary and logical to have an explanatory title and a clear indication of the writer/sender and the recipient.

♣ The language used in report writing should not be informal.

♣ Bullet points and sub-headings are regular features of formal reports, but make sure that they are not just employed as cheap tricks. You have to write something substantial and sustained, not merely drop in a few easy features of layout.

♣ The whole point of most reports is that the provider of the report is advising a body of people to take certain action(s) based on argument and evidence. Therefore, most reports end with a summary or a set of recommendations, often in list form.

Now complete the following:

♣ **Consider everything that has been covered in this section and complete the task: 'Write a report to the head of your school or college from the student committee, suggesting how to organize the annual Open Day. Your report should argue how the school or college needs to appear attractive to prospective students and parents, and also how money can be raised for the benefit of student facilities.'**

4 Transactional and discursive writing

♦ **Return to your group list of possible report tasks and choose one that you feel strongly about. Write the report for a specific audience of your choice. Remember that, despite your strong feelings, you must argue in a controlled, factual way. This is not opinion writing!**

Write your report 'against the clock' in about 30 minutes. It should be between one and two sides of A4 paper.

Speeches

To write a speech you need to consider carefully the points you want to cover and the arguments you will make. In the examination you will be given a topic to discuss, and you will also usually be given a specific audience to write for.

> *Below are some examples of the sorts of speech that you may be asked to write in the examination:*
>
> Write a speech for your fellow students in favour of raising the age limit for driving to 21.
>
> Write your contribution to a national radio phone-in on the use of animals in the circus.
>
> Write your contribution to a radio phone-in on the use of cigarette companies as sponsors for sporting events.

The key to writing speeches is to stay focused on both the topic and your audience.

At the formal end of speech writing is the set-piece contribution to a debate, anything from an organized event in a classroom to a debate in the United Nations. Much less formal is a contribution to a radio phone-in, which is a popular way for people to express their views on a topical issue. In any of these situations, it is of vital importance that your written expression (as well as your voice) is clear, because in the 'real world' you will probably only have one chance to get your views across.

You can use 'I' and 'me' when writing your speech, and also use evidence from your own experience to support your comments. However, speeches should be written in a formal tone using standard English.

Group work

In pairs or small groups, make lists of topics on which a speech could be written. Consider which would be of personal interest to you, which would appeal to particular groups of students, and which would be a fair challenge for all students.

Open your speech with a welcome to your listeners and introduction to the topic. You should summarize the issues you will be discussing.

Read the following opening in response to: *'Write a speech for your fellow students in favour of raising the age limit for driving to 21.'*

> Good afternoon.
>
> Thousands of people are killed or injured on our roads every year because of careless or reckless driving. Many of these accidents are caused by drivers under the age of 21. The legal age limit for driving is currently 17 and many people believe that this is too young. Teenage drivers are viewed as more impulsive, less experienced, less sensible and take more risks than drivers in their twenties. There is strong evidence to suggest that this is in fact true. Male teenage drivers tend to be seen as 'boy racers' and speed around recklessly in their cars with the windows down and their music blaring. There is also the relatively new phenomenon of 'girl racers'. Female teenagers who were previously seen as more sensible drivers have now adopted the dangerous driving habits of their male counterparts. This will not be popular with most of my audience, but I believe that the only solution is to raise the age limit for driving from 17 to 21.

In this speech, the writer introduces the topic of the legal age for driving and opens the argument convincingly. The writer could now go on to discuss the differences in the way teenagers and other drivers use the road, the risks to other drivers, the risks to pedestrians and even the connection between the increase in teenagers drinking alcohol and how this affects their driving habits.

Now complete the following task:
- **Write the opening paragraph for: 'Write a speech to be given to fellow students against raising the age limit for driving to 21.'**

4 Transactional and discursive writing

Often the point of view of a speech will not be given and you will have to express your own point of view through your writing.

Read the following in response to: *'Write a speech for the general public either for or against professional boxing.'*

> Boxing is viewed by many people as a barbaric sport that results in unnecessary injury and death. The instant reaction from the public is often that boxing should be banned. However, what are the consequences of making boxing illegal? I was one of the people who used to believe that boxing should be banned. I have recently changed my mind and come to the conclusion that it is a necessary evil of our society.
>
> If boxing were banned, would this stop boxing matches from taking place? Fights would still occur, but they would be 'underground' in dirty, secret locations. Any injuries suffered during the fights would possibly go untreated because the boxers would fear prosecution if they went to the hospital for medical help. The fights would become more dangerous and deaths would increase because the matches would be unregulated by the rules that govern legal fights now.

This writer states his point of view clearly and even explains that originally he was of the opinion that boxing should be banned. Now it is clear that he is in favour of legalized boxing matches. However, it is possible of course to argue the opposite case – the case against professional boxing.

Now complete the following task:
- **Write a speech for the general public with the opposite point of view to the one above. Argue the case that professional boxing should be banned.**

To conclude your speech, you should summarize the points you have covered, with possible solutions to any problems discussed. For example, here is a possible conclusion to the pro-boxing argument presented above.

> Although professional boxing is incredibly dangerous, to ban it would not prevent people from fighting. More deaths and injuries would result from unregulated matches. The solution is to make the rules that currently govern boxing more strict. Punches to the face and head should be banned, which would hopefully prevent the participants from suffering from severe head injuries or death.

Conventions of speech writing

- Most formal speeches are prepared and written in full detail, so that the person delivering the speech can proceed confidently while in full possession of his or her material. Professional broadcasters and politicians generally read from an autocue – a device that runs through their text at the appropriate speed for them to speak effectively.

- Phone-ins are less formal. However, it might be considered wise for listeners ringing up and finding themselves suddenly 'on-air' to have their thoughts ready in writing. The trick is to appear as if you are NOT reading but are speaking naturally and 'off the cuff'.

- Rhetoric is the traditional word that describes the techniques of speech making. Rhetorical questions (those spoken largely for dramatic effect), and strong repetition of key phrases, are two common techniques. In the end, though, clarity is everything – and overused rhetoric can appear false and corny!

- Certain features of spoken English are not needed in formal speech writing – for instance, fillers like 'er' and 'um'.

- Punctuation has a critical role in speech writing. Well-judged punctuation will slow down the delivery of the speech for the benefit of the listener, who will normally have only one opportunity to digest the contents of the speech.

Now complete the following:

- **Consider everything that has been covered in this unit. Write a speech to be made to fellow students either for or against women going back to work once they have had a baby.**

- **Return to your group list and choose one of the ideas. Write a speech on this topic as a contribution to a national radio phone-in.**

Write one to two sides of A4 paper. Plan, write and check the speech 'against the clock' in about 30 minutes.

Exam tips

- Good transactional writing depends on the writer having a clear sense of purpose, audience and format.
- Pay attention to the specific points raised for each transactional form in the 'Conventions' sections of this unit.
- If your writing task is a direct follow-on to a topic covered by reading material in Section A of Paper 2, do not copy chunks of material from those texts. You should have developed some ideas of your own from your close reading.
- Make sure your writing is accurate. Be very careful with your basic skills and general presentation. Use Unit 4.3 at the end of this section to help you with your technical accuracy.

4 Transactional and discursive writing

Writing to analyse, review, comment

Discursive writing

When preparing and writing a piece of discursive writing, as in transactional writing, the writer generally has a clear point of view to put across to the reader(s). Discursive writing mostly aims to **analyse**, **review** or **comment** on something, and is usually in the form of an article or review.

When writing pieces like these, consider the:
- ♣ purpose – why you are writing
- ♣ audience – who you are writing for.

Articles and reviews

Writing an article for a newspaper or magazine generally requires your opinions on a subject, as well as information about it. It is acceptable to express strong likes or dislikes OR to take a more balanced, reflective view.

Importantly, an article differs from a newspaper report, because a report deals primarily with an account of an event or incident immediately after it has happened. An article is a piece of writing in which to some extent the writer *analyses* (examines in detail), *reviews* (reflects by looking back thoughtfully) and *comments* (offers opinions).

One particular type of newspaper or magazine article is a review, normally understood to be a critical appraisal of a particular book, play, film, etc. However, more general reviews are popular at key points in the calendar, such as an annual review of the best TV newcomers, for example, or an end-of-the-season football review.

> *Here are some examples of the sorts of article and review that you might be asked to write in the exam:*
>
> Write an article for the school magazine discussing the options for students once they have completed their GCSEs.
>
> Write an article for a travel magazine that describes the attractions of a place of your choice.
>
> Write a magazine article **reviewing** one aspect of 'Life in the nineties'. You might like to choose your topic from one of the following: music, fashion, sport, film and television.

Before you begin to write, always consider the context of a piece of writing and show a grasp of the task – its purpose and its intended audience. Adopt an appropriate style and tone. The article or review could be written in a lively and informal way, but a more serious approach could equally be valid. It depends on the situation, the context.

Format is not a major issue in article and review writing. A title or headline is a positive feature, but columns are an unnecessary design feature in the writing process. Again, sub-headings may help the writer, but they are not vital. A fluent piece of continuous prose is the main requirement.

In the following pages you will be shown contrasting writing approaches to deal with the example tasks listed on page 117. In each case, the opening to the writing sets the tone of the whole piece. You will also have the opportunity to try different angles for yourself.

Group work

In pairs or small groups, make lists of topics on which you could write a newspaper or magazine article. Consider which ones would be of strong personal interest to you, which ones would appeal to a particular group of students, and which ones would offer a fair challenge to all students.

When beginning your article, you could compose a clear introduction which includes all of the issues that you will be writing about.

Read the following opening paragraph, written in response to: *'Write an article for the school magazine discussing the options for students once they have completed their GCSEs.'* It is a skilful, balanced introduction to the task.

> There are many opportunities available for students of all abilities once they have completed their GCSEs. For those students interested in completing 'A' Levels, they could either attend a sixth form college or stay on at their current school. For those students who did not achieve high grades, they could attend one of the many specialized courses available that offer on-the-job training. These range from technical skills or engineering-based courses to courses that teach beauty and fashion.

Here the writer adopts a serious, informative tone. S/he takes a neutral position, neither supporting outright the idea of staying on at school, nor suggesting strongly that students should head for college or get a job.

In this article, the writer has introduced the topic and given the relevant areas that the article will be covering. These include:
- options for students who achieved high grades in their GCSEs
- options for students who achieved low grades in their GCSEs
- opportunities for staying on at school
- opportunities for attending college
- opportunities for completing on-the-job training.

4 Transactional and discursive writing

An alternative approach would be to deliberately adopt a point of view, possibly (but not necessarily) your own view. The following introduction adopts a much more obvious 'student-to-student' voice.

> It's that time of year – when thoughts of settling down to exam revision are interrupted by panic attacks over what you are going to do next September! Well, don't go rushing for the holiday brochures 'in denial' – read on ... and discover that the answer to your problem is close to home, right under your nose, in fact. Stay on in the Sixth Form!

This approach could hardly be more different from the first. Note the following contrasts:

ITEM	FIRST OPENING	SECOND OPENING
Opening sentence	Very clear and explicit	Deliberately puzzling
Tone	Fairly formal, serious	Chatty, informal
Sense of audience	Adults, including students	Students
Purpose	Informative, factual	Persuasive, opinionated

As responses to the task, both are well written and equally valid in their approaches. In terms of technical accuracy and consistent tone, both are very successful. You may though prefer one or the other – you may, for example, find the first one dry and stuffy, but you may also find the second one irritating! You might easily find a different way of doing it yourself.

Now do the following:
- **Begin your own response to the same task: 'Write an article for the school magazine discussing the options for students once they have completed their GCSEs.'**

Complete at least two paragraphs – you may well choose to argue passionately in favour of college or the world of work.

When you've finished the above task, have a go at the one below – using any approach with which you feel comfortable.
- **Write the opening two paragraphs of a response to this task: 'Write an article for the school magazine discussing the ways that the school can be more environmentally friendly.'**

Sometimes the point of view you need to take is given to you in the wording of the task. In cases like this, the critical decision that you have to make is about the content you will use to put across that point of view. For example, in a task such as: *'Write an article for a travel magazine that describes the attractions of a place of your choice'*, you can interpret 'place' to suit your own needs.

Read the following piece which achieves a broad sweep across South Wales, sharing a sense of history and regional geography with the reader.

In South Wales there are many attractions, ranging from old castles to modern art, and sport and leisure facilities. Although South Wales used to be a coal mining area and thick black smoke used to fill the air, now it is virtually unspoilt and is home to some of the most breathtaking natural scenery in Great Britain. South Wales is famous for its valleys, and the mountains that surround these offer plenty of opportunities for walking, hiking and exploring. Many of these mountains are covered with thick forests that are home to a wide range of bird and animal species. The Brecon Beacons, Wales' national park, is famous for its beautiful waterfalls.

Equally, you might choose to write with sharper focus on one particular place, with or without close descriptive knowledge of it.

Cardiff is Europe's youngest capital city and it is indeed a place for the young. 'Cool Cymru' has its heart here in the bright, pedestrianised shopping areas and the city centre parks and squares. From mid-morning to late at night, there is a vibrant, friendly atmosphere for the visitor to enjoy. Somehow, you are never far from the sounds of the Manic Street Preachers, the Stereophonics and a new generation of Welsh musical talent. Cardiff's pride and joy, of course, is the Millennium Stadium, bang in the middle of the city centre ...

It obviously helps if you choose a busy location to write about, but the important thing is to think about your choice and find something a little bit personal and individual to write. You could, therefore, quite sensibly choose to write about a small, remote village, provided you are able to focus on two or three features that make the place what it is – local characters, an annual event, an early morning scene, perhaps. If you judge that you do not have that kind of material, think again and land on another, maybe broader choice.

Now complete the following:

* **Write your own response to the same task: 'Write an article for a travel magazine that describes the attractions of a place of your choice.'**

You are writing for a travel magazine so think about your audience. You can then tailor your writing to inform and interest them, and make them want to visit the place or area of your choice.

Try not to display a totally negative attitude in your articles. Here is a task that tests your willingness to be positive: *'Write an article for a women's magazine discussing what life is like for teenagers in the 21st century.'*

NOTE Older adults, as well as teenagers, follow GCSE English courses, and they may well have something to say along the lines of 'You've never had it so good!'

4 Transactional and discursive writing

Below is a possible opening paragraph that may prompt a few thoughts of your own. It treads carefully, not attempting to take sides, either for or against teenagers today. You may have stronger views, but, whatever they are, try to write about the topic in a mature way.

In the 21st century, life is very different to the way it was even 50 years ago. There have been significant improvements to every aspect of teenagers' lives. Teenagers' free time is dominated by music, films and going out with their friends. Girls spend a lot of their time shopping for the latest fashions, which teenagers feel compelled to keep up with, and chatting with their friends. Boys tend to spend their free time either playing or watching sports. Despite all of the anxieties that usually go with the teenage years, it is generally a happy time.

Now complete the following:

* **Write your own response to the same task 'Write an article for a women's magazine discussing what life is like for teenagers in the 21st century.' As before, think about your audience and the purpose of your article.**

Having a chance to write about a topic of your choice in an exam is a great opportunity. The turn of the millennium was an obvious time for looking backwards as well as forwards, and was a chance for this review task to be considered: *'Write a magazine article reviewing one aspect of "Life in the nineties". You might like to choose your topic from one of the following: music, fashion, sport, film and television.'*

Read the following example of someone taking full advantage of this near free-choice opportunity:

Football in the nineties really started when Manchester United marked the return of English clubs to European competition by winning the 1991 European Cup-Winners' Cup in Rotterdam by beating Barcelona 2-1. Five years in the wilderness followed the Heysel Stadium tragedy in 1985, when Juventus fans were trampled to death in a stampede allegedly caused by Liverpool fans. Liverpool suffered again, of course, in 1989 when 90 of their own supporters were crushed in the Hillsborough disaster.

So a new era started with our clubs back in Europe and a brand-new squeaky clean Premier League with all-seater stadiums. Top players began to earn obscene wages, but the product was brilliant and players from all over the world flocked to England as the main attraction …

… By the end of the decade, TV was saturated with football and even women's football was gaining a higher profile. Oh yes, and the decade ended with Manchester United becoming the first British club to win the European Champions League.

The expertise of this writer shines through very quickly. There is also a very clever structure to the writing, with the whole piece framed by the two references to Manchester United as well as the key themes of money, safety and football as a world sport. It is a rather 'blokish' example, some might think, but who says that it was written by a man?

The review task above makes the student fully responsible for the content of the piece. You should be ready to respond to this kind of opportunity, which is not unique to the above task. Your GCSE course and this unit of work should help to give you the confidence to 'think on your feet' during an examination.

Now complete the following:

♣ **Write a review for a topical magazine targeted at young people – EITHER a review that focuses on one item (for example, a film or a TV programme) OR a review that looks back over the previous year in some area of interest to you (for example, music, sport, fashion).**

♣ **Return to your group list of possible newspaper and magazine articles. Choose one topic and write an interesting and enjoyable article for a general interest magazine for people of all ages. Remember your article should be informative as well as expressing your personal views.**

Write about two sides of A4 paper 'against the clock' in about 30 minutes.

Exam tips

- Be prepared to respond to an *'analyse, review, comment'* task on something very specific, but also on something much more general. DO NOT write prepared articles, but be ready with a range of topics that you can respond to thoughtfully and promptly.
- Think like a journalist, who also has to write under pressure. Focus on the situation at hand and think of an angle that will start you off and allow you to develop an interesting personal response.
- Think about why you are writing and who you are writing for.
- Make sure your writing is accurate. Be very careful with your basic skills and general presentation. Use Unit 4.3 at the end of this section to help you with your technical accuracy.

Technical accuracy in transactional and discursive writing

Technical accuracy in transactional and discursive writing is crucially important for successful communication. In the real world, your opinions in writing may not be taken seriously if there are blatant weaknesses in your expression. Errors in spelling will prove to be a distraction for your reader and imprecise punctuation and grammar will prevent you from making crisp, persuasive arguments. Muddled sentences, meanwhile, will confuse your audience.

Listed below are criteria for achieving the best performance in sentence structure, punctuation and spelling at GCSE:

- appropriate and effective **variation of sentence structure**
- sophisticated use of **simple**, **compound and complex sentences** to achieve particular effects
- use of **accurate punctuation** to vary pace, clarify meaning, avoid ambiguity and create deliberate effects
- virtually all **spelling correct**, including that of complex irregular words
- confident and purposeful use of **verb tenses** and correct **grammatical agreement**.

This unit works in conjunction with Unit 2.3 (Technical accuracy in descriptive and imaginative writing), and the criteria listed above are also valid for descriptive and imaginative writing. It offers further areas for close consideration, focusing especially on those features of language that are characteristic of transactional and discursive writing. Again, technical terms are kept to a minimum and they do not have to be learned!

Read the following extracts from students' writing in exams. The emphasis is on quality at word level and sentence level, so there has been no attempt to lay out the extracts realistically.

TRAVEL WRITING: an idealized view of London

It is a cliché, but it's true. London has it all. It's not surprising it is one of the most famous cities in the world, renowned for its huge department stores, exclusive boutiques, and beautiful historical monuments. London has so much to offer. It has something for everyone. It is a vibrant city, brimming with life, and it is possible to spend days wandering through London, just watching life happen around you. There are many huge department stores, including the world-famous Harrods, full of the latest designer collections; there are also many quaint markets where you can hunt out amazing bargains and take in the atmosphere of traditional market life ...

TRAVEL WRITING: *an alternative guide*

... For all those people who wish to have their romantic image of Suffolk – rolling fields, country ale and slightly simple locals – shattered, Lowestoft is the place to go.

It is inevitably a grey day, as you drive along the road running parallel to the pier. The sea and the sky have seemingly merged into a grey mass, yet the beach is packed with holidaymakers showing off their 'Dunkirk Spirit', as they resolutely continue their holidays amidst the horrible conditions.

Lowestoft: the seafront reeks of greasy fish-and-chips, the arcades are shut for restoration, but the holidaymakers are smiling and enjoying themselves. No matter how horrible the weather is, people come to Lowestoft and enjoy themselves. Please excuse my faintly incredulous tone, but there truly is something about Lowestoft that draws beach-addicts like Glastonbury attracts middle-aged hippies ...

LETTER WRITING: *strong personal views in a formal setting*

I am writing in reply to the letter published last week, regarding the amount of money paid to celebrities. While I agree with your correspondent's views that these people are paid ridiculous amounts of money considering how many needy people there are in the world, I feel a few points need to be clarified ...

... Homelessness and poverty are social problems and, as such, must be dealt with by society as a whole. Pointing the finger at celebrities, overpaid as they are, doesn't solve the problem. No single person can be blamed; these problems arise because of all of us. From overpaid stars who avoid paying taxes to each of us who doesn't put money in charity boxes, we can all be blamed in equal measure ...

SPEECH: *a shared interest – speaking to teenagers about teenagers*

... Vandalism is quite a problem in some areas so there needs to be something done so that those responsible have another thing to occupy their time. Youth clubs in the evening are a very good way of distracting teenagers away from crime and spending time constructively with their friends. However, as I am sure you'll agree, these youth clubs have to be run with a friendly, caring atmosphere or otherwise we won't have an incentive to attend. Youth clubs should be run by people who are in touch with teenagers enough to see what our wants and needs are. Above all, they have to have control, as I think we have all had fun with someone who can't control us. Respect goes both ways and (being a teenager myself) I know that the finger of blame is often pointed at the wrong people, so those running the club need to have respect ...

4 Transactional and discursive writing

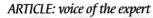

LEAFLET: gentle persuasion

Healthy eating is easily accomplished if you follow a few simple rules – fruit and vegetables are bursting with vitamins that could help you considerably! If you aim to eat five types per day, then you will be fighting fit in no time at all. You should also try to exercise about three times a week (no more than half an hour each time), which is a very small price to pay for your life. If you are concerned that you won't stick to a chocolate-free diet, then do not worry, as that is precisely why diets are formed. If you balance your eating, then a few treats like biscuits and cakes will not stop you achieving your goal ...

SPEECH: committed opposition

I would like to begin by saying that I am vehemently opposed to boxing. I find that it is a barbaric sport, glorifying violence and blood with little moral or social justification.

The supporters of boxing say that they are merely fans of sport, and that they enjoy the art and technique in the sport. I am afraid that I disagree with this – a boxing audience's main interest is in the gratuitous violence and testosterone-fuelled machismo which compels one man to hit another ...

... I would like to conclude by making this point – we cannot continue to hide behind the fact that illegal boxing is dangerous when it is blatantly obvious that legalized boxing is not only dangerous but damaging, demeaning, and ultimately spells death for the participant, while the sport's promoters and managers earn unholy amounts of money, with little or no risk to themselves.

ARTICLE: voice of the expert

Many of the music-lovers around will remember the 1990s as the dance/techno and club music era.

It has been in the past decade, however, that I believe a more positive aspect of music has developed. Producers and artists alike have drastically improved the tacky sound of keyboard synthesizers in the late seventies and the eighties and the musical world now has more live instrument playing and realistic instrument sounds from the advanced music modules, used by many producers.

Take 'The Corrs' for example: this group have made violin playing fashionable once more with their popular violin solos in many of their songs. Groups and artists such as the 'Lighthouse Family', 'Coolio' and 'Bjork' have also helped this and I myself often have my violin pupils asking how to play the latest 'The Corrs' solo ...

Now complete this task:

+ **Discuss the above samples of transactional and discursive writing. Each is a model of good writing at GCSE. Consider each one in turn and identify the features of language and style that make each piece of writing successful.**

It will help if you look closely at:
– the words and phrases used
– the style and structure of sentences chosen
– the sense of purpose and audience (the way the argument or discussion is organized).

Sentence structure

Revision task – simple, compound and complex sentences

The following paragraph about fox-hunting is written in simple sentences of a similar style and length. It does not present a powerful argument because there are so many pauses in the writing.

* **Re-write the paragraph in a mixture of simple, compound and complex sentences so that it is more interesting to read.**

(If you need to remind yourself of simple, compound and complex sentences, refer back to Unit 2.3.)

> I think fox hunting is cruel. It is unnecessary. It does not control the fox population. It is just a hobby for the wealthy. Fox hunting cannot be called a "sport". A sport is a challenge between equals. There is no equality in a fox running away from a pack of forty hounds and horses and their riders. This is unfair. The fox is almost guaranteed to lose. Where is the sport in that? I think fox hunting should be banned. I am asking you to campaign for fox hunting to be made illegal.

Good writing, such as the samples at the beginning of this unit, uses a combination of sentence lengths and styles. This makes the arguments more readable and more authoritative. The writers sound as though they have carefully considered and planned what they are going to say – and they probably have.

Now read about some key features of more ambitious writing.

KEY FEATURES	EXAMPLES
More complex sentences Complex sentences can express a subtle thought in a precise way – but they have to be controlled. They should be constructed and punctuated thoughtfully. The samples of writing contain many examples of ambitious and successful sentence structure.	* *From overpaid stars who avoid paying taxes to each of us who doesn't put money in charity boxes, we can all be blamed in equal measure.* * *No matter how horrible the weather is, people come to Lowestoft and enjoy themselves.* * *Youth clubs should be run by people who are in touch with teenagers enough to see what our wants and needs are.*
Passive voice The *passive* voice is impersonal and is associated with a *formal* style of writing. The verb is the indicator of the passive voice. Some writing types (e.g. a formal report) require a greater degree of formality than others (e.g. brochure writing). The passive voice adds to the range of sentence styles and can add some sense of authority too.	* *... the finger of blame is often pointed at the wrong people ...* * *Youth clubs should be run by people who ...* * *... we can all be blamed in equal measure ...* * *... these people are paid ridiculous amounts of money ...*

4 Transactional and discursive writing

Indirect (or reported) speech

Indirect speech reports the words or thoughts of a 'speaker'. As in the two sample sentences opposite, this reporting style occurs naturally in transactional and discursive writing, but there are several issues of style, meaning and accuracy to negotiate!

- The supporters of boxing say **that they** are merely fans of sport, **and that they** enjoy the art and technique in the sport.
- I know **that** the finger of blame is often pointed at the wrong people ...

The sentence:
Dick Whittington said, 'The streets of London **are paved** with gold.' (DIRECT SPEECH)
becomes:
Dick Whittington said (that) the streets of London **were paved** with gold. (INDIRECT SPEECH)

Connectives and conjunctions

Connectives and conjunctions are the 'link' words that help good writing to flow. Connectives are words and phrases (like 'however', 'unfortunately', 'in contrast', 'secondly', 'in fact', etc.) that relate a sentence closely to a previous one; conjunctions (like 'if', 'when', 'although', 'so', etc.) are words that actually join sentences together. Note that 'however' (connective) and 'although' (conjunction) are in different categories and cannot simply be interchanged.

- **Above all**, they have to have control ...
- **However**, as I am sure you'll agree, these youth clubs have to be run with a friendly, caring atmosphere ...
- The sea and the sky have seemingly merged into a grey mass, **yet** the beach is packed with holidaymakers showing off their 'Dunkirk Spirit', **as** they resolutely continue their holidays amidst the horrible conditions.
- Take 'The Corrs' **for example**: ...
- **If** you aim to eat five types per day, **then** you will be fighting fit in no time at all. You should **also** try to exercise about three times a week ...
- It is **inevitably** a grey day, **as** you drive along the road running parallel to the pier.

See Unit 2.3 (Technical accuracy in descriptive and imaginative writing) for further support in **sentence structure**, relating to:
- simple sentences
- compound sentences
- complex sentences
- noun phrases
- minor sentences.

Now complete this task:
- **Write a paragraph (or two) arguing whether or not cigarette smoking should be made illegal.**

Remember to vary and control the length and style of your sentences.

Punctuation

In transactional writing, as in imaginative writing, you must try to punctuate your work properly. This means understanding the basic rules and knowing how to use the full range of punctuation and presentation skills.

PUNCTUATION	EXAMPLES
More about commas Commas are an important part of your control of more ambitious complex sentences. Often they work in pairs, acting as a pair of brackets – check by reading back your sentences that the commas are functioning as you wish. Check that they are not just decorative.	♣ *Homelessness and poverty are social problems and, as such, must be dealt with by society as a whole.* ♣ *Pointing the finger at celebrities, overpaid as they are, doesn't solve the problem.* ♣ *It is a vibrant city, brimming with life, and it is possible to spend days wandering through London, just watching life happen around you.*
Apostophes The apostrophe has two identities – the apostrophe of *omission* and the *possessive* apostrophe. **1** An apostrophe of omission replaces missing letters. e.g. *we're, they'll, it's* (it is) There is no break where words 'join', e.g. *didn't*. **2** For the possessive apostrophe, a word ends in *'s* or *s'* to show that it is the **owner** of whatever follows it. The apostrophe should always be placed immediately after the exact name of the owner, e.g. *the supporters' club, the team's coach.*	♣ *It is a cliché, but it's true.* ♣ *... your correspondent's view ...* ♣ *... As I am sure you'll agree ...* ♣ *(boxing)...the sport's promoters* NOTE: **Do not** use an apostrophe for a simple plural! **Do not** use words containing the apostrophe of omission for very formal writing types, e.g. reports.
Semi-colons Use semi-colons to join two closely linked sentences, both of which could stand as sentences on their own. Semi-colons can also be used (instead of commas) to separate the items within a complicated list introduced by a colon or dash.	♣ *There are many huge department stores, including the world-famous Harrods, full of the latest designer collections; there are also many quaint markets ...* ♣ *No single person can be blamed; these problems arise because of all of us.*
Colons (or dashes) *Colons* serve the very useful purpose of providing a major pause within a sentence, sometimes to introduce a list. The *dash* can acceptably replace the colon.	♣ *Take 'The Corrs' for example: this group have made violin playing fashionable once more ...* ♣ *Lowestoft: the seafront reeks of greasy fish-and-chips, the arcades are shut for restoration ...* ♣ *Healthy eating is easily accomplished if you follow a few simple rules – fruit and vegetables are bursting with vitamins that could help you considerably!*

Brackets/dashes (in pairs)

These are very useful sometimes for adding supplementary or non-essential information to a sentence.

- *You should also try to exercise about three times a week (no more than half an hour each time), which is a very small price to pay for your life.*
- *Respect goes both ways and (being a teenager myself) I know that the finger of blame is often pointed at the wrong people ...*
- *For all those people who wish to have their romantic image of Suffolk – rolling fields, country ale and slightly simple locals – shattered, Lowestoft is the place to go.*

Paragraphs

Paragraphs give shape to a piece of writing and help the reader's eyes move around the page easily. Paragraphs (identifiable through indentations or a blank line) operate as a form of **punctuation beyond the sentence**. See each paragraph as a digestible chunk of reading.

There is no strict rule about when to start a new paragraph, but each one should start with a key sentence, called a topic sentence.

Generally, in most forms of writing, paragraphs should be of roughly even length, typically perhaps between three and six sentences.

Leaflets, brochures and some newspaper reports sometimes have very short paragraphs. This is usually a design feature, created so that key text catches the eye. Ask yourself the question – is there shape and consistency to the piece of writing you are working on?

See Unit 2.3 (Technical accuracy in descriptive and imaginative writing) for further support in **punctuation**, relating to:
- full stops
- capital letters
- commas
- question marks
- exclamation marks
- speech marks.

Now complete this task:

- **Write the opening paragraph (or two) of a speech discussing the claim that there is too much violence on television.**

Pay particular attention to punctuation, including dramatic pauses (possibly represented by dashes).

Spelling

Complete the following task:

◆ **Study the samples of writing at the beginning of this unit and compile lists of examples of each of the following categories of spelling:**
- **homophones**
- **vowel choices**
- **double consonants**
- **irregular plurals**
- **word endings**
- **silent letters**
- **polysyllabic words.**

Refer, if necessary, to the spelling notes in the grid on page 63 (Unit 2.3) and make representative lists in the same way.

Grammar

KEY FEATURES	EXAMPLES
Pronouns A pronoun is a word that stands in place of a noun. There are several categories of pronoun and there is a range of common errors. For example: *Him and me have changed our minds.* ✗ *She disagreed with he and I.* ✗ *If you are serious, one must do something.* ✗ *He discussed the matter with myself.* ✗ *The person which ...* ✗ Spellings: *hisself* ✗ *theirselves* ✗	◆ *... people come to Lowestoft and enjoy **themselves**.* ◆ *From overpaid stars **who** avoid paying taxes to **each of us who** doesn't put money in charity boxes, we can all be blamed in equal measure.* ◆ *If **you** balance your eating, then a few treats like biscuits and cakes will not stop **you** achieving your goal ...*
Comparatives and superlatives A lot of common errors occur with comparatives and superlatives ... and some of them are fairly ugly! You should be able to work out what is wrong with the following examples and what the rules are for *-er* and *-est*. *... more richer ...* ✗ *... worser and worser ...* ✗ *... bestest ...* ✗ *... most handsomest ...* ✗ *... comfortabler ...* ✗ *... intelligenter ...* ✗ *... more quick ...* ✗	◆ *one of **the most famous** cities in the world* ◆ *a **more positive** aspect of music* A *comparative adjective* acts as a comparison between two items. A *superlative adjective* compares more than two items. For example: *Even though the game ended in a draw, England for once seemed the **better** team.* ✓ *Overall however, Australia are still the **best** team in the world.* ✓ It is perhaps worth learning the following sequences: *good ... better ... best* *bad ... worse ... worst* *some ... more ... most* *some ... less ... least*

Prepositions

A preposition is a word or phrase that shows the relationship between two parts of a sentence, often of time or place. Prepositions are key grammatical words in all kinds of writing, from the simplest positional example of description (e.g. *on* the table) to complex abstractions of argument and discussion (e.g. disapproved *of*, in opposition *to*).

- ♣ *It is a vibrant city, brimming **with** life, and it is possible to spend days wandering **through** London, just watching life happen **around** you.*
- ♣ *Lowestoft: the seafront reeks **of** greasy fish-and-chips, the arcades are shut **for** restoration ...*
- ♣ *I am writing **in** reply **to** the letter published last week, regarding the amount **of** money paid **to** celebrities.*

Agreement

Grammatical agreement is an ever-present requirement in standard English, especially in writing. In any sentence, each word must agree grammatically with the other words in the sentence. Lack of grammatical agreement is at the heart of many mistakes in English.

We was is a common agreement error – the verb *was* does not agree with the subject *we*.

The boy done good contains two agreement errors – the verb should be *did* or *has done* and the adjective *good* should be an adverb *well*.

As noted earlier, pronouns and also comparative and superlative adjectives suffer from agreement errors: *The families enjoyed ourselves even though it was the worse weather of the summer*. In this example, *themselves* and *worst* are needed for grammatical agreement.

We is ... ✗   They was ... ✗   I does ... ✗   You is ... ✗   We comes ... ✗
... danced good ... ✗   ... played bad ... ✗   ... sang great ... ✗   ... writes quick ... ✗
... them girls ... ✗   ... the man what we saw ... ✗   ... please see myself ... ✗

At a more complex level, there is an agreement issue that is less clear. Collective nouns like *government* or *crowd* or *family* can be seen as singular or plural, depending on circumstances:
The crowd <u>was</u> very large. ✓   *The crowd <u>were</u> all raising their hands, 'doing the wave'.* ✓

Verbs

A verb is a word (or a group of words) that indicates an **action** or a **state of being**.

It is impossible to cover adequately the complexity of verbs in a unit that deals with technical accuracy in general. However, verbs are the heart of every sentence, so it would be foolish to underestimate their importance to your writing.

Here are some key areas to consider:

Verb tenses: past, present, future and several subtle variations
PAST: We **visited** Birmingham yesterday. We **have visited** four cities in the last two days.
PRESENT: Today we **visit** Nottingham. We **are visiting** Nottingham at the moment.
FUTURE: We **are going to visit** Sheffield soon. Tomorrow we **will visit** Sheffield.

Regular verbs These appear in four different forms – ***base*** (or ***infinitive***) -s -ing -ed

walk	walks	walking	walked	
try	tries	trying	tried	(Regular -ed, but note spelling pattern)

Irregular verbs There are many other verbs that do not behave as you would expect, e.g. *I digged* ✗   *I dug* ✓

send	sends	sending	sent	(Verbs with a past tense ending in -t)
shut	shuts	shutting	shut	(Verbs with an unchanging past tense)
win	wins	winning	won	(Verbs with a changed vowel sound)
choose	chooses	choosing	chose/chosen	(Verbs with different forms of past tense)

Auxiliary verbs: These three verbs support the others, e.g. *I **do** <u>think</u> that he **has been** <u>lying</u>.*

be	am, are, is	being	was, were, been
do	do, does	doing	did, done
have	have, has	having	had

Modal verbs

Modal verbs are verbs that offer subtle shades of meaning of *possibility*, *permission* and *obligation*. For example:
can   may   will   shall   must   could   might   would   should
They are straightforward to list but rather harder to use with confidence.

Active voice and passive voice (see the notes on 'passive voice' under 'Sentence structure')

ACTIVE: Trevor Macdonald reads the news.
PASSIVE: The news is read by Trevor Macdonald.

Moods of verbs

INDICATIVE: Cardiff is Europe's youngest capital city.   (statement)
INTERROGATIVE: What should we do to combat vandalism?   (question)
IMPERATIVE: Answer both questions in this section.   (command)
SUBJUNCTIVE: If I were Prime Minister, I would ...   (conditional sentence)

Now complete this task:

♣ **Write a formal report about improving discipline and behaviour to the headteacher/principal from the point of view of students in your year group.**

Consider everything that has been covered in Section 4 as you write your piece. Try to make your writing as formal as possible – you are representing the views of your colleagues, not stating your own opinions.

TIP Before you start, look back at Unit 4.1 to remind yourself of the conventions of report writing.

Final task

If you eliminate careless errors from your writing, your grade is bound to improve. The students who have written the pieces below display a mixture of promise and self-destruction!

◆ **Discuss the weaknesses of each of the following extracts. Rewrite each of them, correcting the errors and improving the vocabulary and style.**

1

I am replying to your intrest for a new part time employee at your hotel. I am very intrested at the position and would like to tell you more on myself.

I live in _____, it is about twenty minutes away from your hotel. I have a car and so it wouldn't be much problem getting to and from work. I am willing to work any hours offered to me. I will work Saturdays but I would like Sundays off. Last summer I worked for the _____ hotel in Cornwall. I did all jobs available there. I worked on reception in the kitchen and as a life guard at the pool. I have a life guard citificate and a reference which I have enclosed in the letter.

2

I have decided to write you a letter asking you to put a ban whaling all around the world because I have been reading things about what happened to the animals and I think you should have a read and see for yourself

I think this because I found out that by the end of the year all the whales and dolphins could be extinked. I was looking at some pictures of the whales and dolphins when they where being hunted polluted by the chemical factories in the area and trapped in the fishing nets where they will soon drown in.

3

I can't remember everything over the last ten years but I remember a lot. At the begining of the 90s the music wasn't that great from what I can remember but as time went by the music started to get better and people started to like it. people always wore fashionable clothes because they didn't want to feel different from everyone else. The sporting events have nealy all been the same for the last ten years but more people are starting to play sports like football, tennis, hockey and ice hocky but there are a lot more sports being played now then at the beginning of the 90s. a lot of people like to watch television or even watch a video there are a lot more films and tv programs on the telly now then there was at the beginning of the 90s and a lot more people have got televisions because not many people had tvs untill the late 1990s. there are a lot of computers around now then their was before because not many people could aford them but people, get more money now so more people buy them. That was some information about the 90s that I could remember.

4

I'm replying to a letter I read in the daily mail on Wednesday about British being, animal lovers. Or not, is how it seems!

The letter states that the British are supposed to be a nation of animal lovers, this statement I think is wrong. It's not that we are 'supposed' to be. We choose to be animal lovers and the majority of us are. There are a few British who aren't animal lovers but that's they're choise, noone can be forced to be something they are not.

5

I think that people who are cruel to domestic pets and farm animals should be ashamed of themselves because they are domestic pets and they chose to have them, so they should feed them, clean them and treat them good and not be cruel to them. If they don'' want their pets anymore they should give them to someone that do or phone the pet rescue centre.

Exam tips

- Think and plan (in your head) before you write.
- Give attention to the format and layout of your writing.
- Write in standard English and judge as you plan your response to a task just how formal you need to be.
- Write to the recommended length for each task, but don't go beyond it. Quality, not quantity!
- Check your work at the end of each task for silly errors.

4 Transactional and discursive writing

English literature

Sections A and B (each 30%) will require candidates to answer two questions on the chosen prose text and two questions on the chosen drama text. The first question will require close reading of an extract. The second question will offer a choice of tasks relating to the text as a whole.

Section C (10%) will consist of a question offering some structure for candidates to explore and respond to a single unseen poem.

Sections A and B (each 26%) will require candidates to answer two questions on the prose and poetry sections of the anthology respectively. The first question will require close reading of a prose extract/poem. The second question will offer a choice of tasks relating to the prose/poetry section as a whole and involving the comparison of short stories and poems respectively.

Section C (18%) will require candidates to answer one question (18%) on the chosen drama text. This will offer a choice of tasks relating to the text as a whole.

The study of literature centres on an informed personal response to a range of texts in the genres of prose, poetry and drama. There is some flexibility in the choice of texts to be studied and overlap with GCSE English is positively encouraged.

In English Literature the criteria being assessed are:
a knowledge and interpretation of text
b exploring language, structure and form
c conveying response
d making comparisons (Specification B written paper*)

This section of the book contains five units:
5.1 Responding to extracts You will closely read extracts from set texts.
5.2 Discursive essay questions You will learn how to write discursive pieces on set texts.
5.3 Empathy questions You will learn how to write empathic pieces on set texts.
5.4 Poetry appreciation You will learn how to explore and respond to a single poem.
5.5 Anthology comparison tasks (prose and poetry) You will learn how to write comparative pieces on anthology texts (Specification B only).

* In English Literature Specification A, this criterion is assessed in coursework.

> (Read the extract, then answer the questions following it:)
>
> Look closely at how ____ is presented here. How does it affect your feelings towards him/her?
>
> With close reference to the extract, show how the writer suggests ____'s feelings here.
>
> With close reference to the extract, show how ____ creates mood and atmosphere here.
>
> What does this extract reveal about the characters of ____ and ____?
>
> **(i)** What thoughts and feelings do you have as you read this extract?
>
> **(ii)** Choose parts of the extract that you find particularly effective and write about them, explaining why you find them effective.

When you first see the prose or drama extract, read it through carefully. There will be many things to consider as you read the extract, such as the characters, the dialogue, the action and the descriptions.

You need to focus on the extract. Where does it occur in the novel or play? What has happened before? What happens after the extract? Most importantly, what happens in the extract?

Prose and drama: questions for both genres

PROSE and DRAMA both have **characters, relationships, mood** and **atmosphere**. They also have **plot** and **setting**.

Both the drama and prose tasks will focus on similar aspects of the extract. You need to understand what the question is asking for and how to respond to it appropriately.

Questions about characters

Characters are revealed by:
- what they say, think, feel and do
- how they are described
- what others say, think and feel about them; how they act towards them.

> What does this extract reveal about the character(s) ____?
>
> Show how the writer demonstrates ____'s thoughts and feelings here.
>
> What are your thoughts and feelings as you read this extract?

In answering, consider some or all of the following:

- Do the character(s) speak and behave in ways that are consistent with their behaviour in the rest of the novel or play?
- Do they say or do anything surprising? How do they say and do these things?
- How do others react?
- What are the characters' motives and intentions? What do they want to do or what do they want to get?
- Do these motives and intentions match what is being said and done?
- What is the character's current state of mind? How does this change? What **exactly** changes it?
- How does the character feel about other characters, about what they say and do?
- What **exactly** makes the characters think and feel this way?
- Do the characters' feelings change? In what way(s)?
- How do you feel about the characters? Is your opinion different for each of them?
- What emotions do you experience as you read the extract? Do these emotions change?
- What **exactly** makes you feel this way?

Part of model answer

... The reader sees the immense grief that Silas will experience. When the truth sets in, his physical reaction becomes almost shocking to the reader: 'trembling more and more'. When Silas shakes so much that he drops the candle it symbolizes any previous joy and luxury in his miserable life being extinguished. All light is put out (the gold in his life taken.) It is hard not to feel quite sad for him ...

Now complete the following task:

- **Choose an appropriate extract from one of your prescribed texts and write a few lines about the main character in the extract.**

Questions about relationships

Relationships are revealed by:
- what characters say to each other and how they say it
- how they act towards each other
- how they feel and think about each other.

> What does this extract reveal about the relationship between   and   ?

In answering, consider some or all of the following:

- What do the characters say to each other?
- How are these things said? Are they said in a friendly way? In a sarcastic way? In an aggressive way?

- What is being implied by what is said? Is it easy to understand how these characters feel about each other? Is it difficult to determine how they feel? Why?
- How do the characters behave with each other?
- What does their body language reveal?
- What do other characters say about their relationship?
- How do you feel about their relationship? Does your attitude change? Why?
- Does their relationship change? What **exactly** changes it?

Part of model answer

... Lennie looks up to George, so much so that he 'imitated him exactly'. George seems to be the sole influence in Lennie's life so he wants to be the same as him. He likes to seek acceptance and approval from George, so he adjusts his hat precisely so that it was 'the way George's hat was' ...

Now complete the following task:
- **Choose another appropriate extract from one of your prescribed texts and write a few lines about the relationship between the main characters in the extract.**

Questions about mood and atmosphere

Show how the writer creates mood and atmosphere in this extract.

In answering, you need to focus on the way the writer has written the extract.
- Where is the extract based? Is it in a dark wood? A brightly lit classroom? A castle? An office? A garage?
- How does the location of the extract affect the behaviour of the characters? Are they unhappy? Scared? Depressed? Tired? Bored?
- What sounds does the writer describe in the background? Is there noisy machinery? Thunder and lightning? Running water? Chatter?
- How do these noises affect the characters?
- How do the characters speak? Are they angry? Frightened? Amazed? Excited?
- How do the characters behave? Are they nervous? Confident? Aggressive? Romantic?
- How does the passage make you feel as you read it? Do you feel the same way as the characters or do you feel different? Why is this?
- What is the overall effect of the passage? How do you feel when you have finished reading it?

Part of model answer

... In the second paragraph of the extract, George Eliot reinforces the sense of distress and loneliness that Silas feels. This part is very emotional, with the onomatopoeic effect of the word 'moaned' allowing the reader to actually hear Silas's pain ...

Now complete the following task:

♣ **Choose another appropriate extract from one of your prescribed texts and write a few lines about the mood and atmosphere in the extract.**

Prose: questions for prose texts only

PROSE has **readers**. It also has **descriptions, paragraphs, chapters** and a **narrator**.

Because novels are written to be read (unlike drama, which is written to be performed), you may be asked a question concerning the reader.

Questions about the reader

How does this extract influence the reader's attitudes towards ___ ?

To answer this type of question, you need to consider the impact the extract has on you.

Think about some or all of the following:
♣ Is there narration/description that influences your attitude?
♣ Do the characters behave in typical or untypical ways? Do they surprise you?
♣ What do they say? How do they say it? How does this affect you?
♣ How does the extract make you feel? Do you feel angry? Sad? Satisfied? Excited? Happy? Shocked?
♣ How do you feel half way through the extract?
♣ How do you feel at the end of the extract?
♣ Do your thoughts and feelings about the characters change?
♣ How do they change? Why do they change? When do they change?
♣ What specific incidents did you react to? Why?

A prose extract

Read the extract from *Hard Times* by Charles Dickens. It follows a sample task, and a student response is provided in full on page 141. Even though you may not be studying this novel, it is quite possible to write about the extract; you may wish to do this, in order to gain experience of tackling prose texts.

Sample task:
♣ **With close reference to the extract, explain how this extract influences the thoughts and feelings of the reader.**

HARD TIMES
Charles Dickens

Old Stephen descended the two white steps, shutting the black door with the brazen door-plate, by the aid of the brazen full-stop, to which he gave a parting polish with the sleeve of his coat, observing that his hot hand clouded it. He crossed the street with his eyes bent upon the ground, and thus was walking sorrowfully away, when he felt a touch upon his arm.

It was not the touch he needed most at such a moment – the touch that could calm the wild waters of his soul, as the uplifted hand of the sublimest love and patience could abate the raging of the sea – yet it was a woman's hand too. It was an old woman, tall and shapely still, though withered by time, on whom his eyes fell when he stopped and turned. She was very cleanly and plainly dressed, had country mud upon her shoes, and was newly come from a journey. The flutter of her manner, in the unwonted noise of the streets; the spare shawl, carried unfolded on her arm; the heavy umbrella, and little basket; the loose long-fingered gloves, to which her hands were unused; all bespoke an old woman from the country, in her plain holiday clothes, come into Coketown on an expedition of rare occurrence. Remarking this at a glance, with the quick observation of his class, Stephen Blackpool bent his attentive face – his face, which, like the faces of many of his order, by dint of long working with eyes and hands in the midst of a prodigious noise, had acquired the concentrated look with which we are familiar in the countenances of the deaf – the better to hear what she asked him.

"Pray, Sir," said the old woman, "didn't I see you come out of that gentleman's house?" pointing back to Mr Bounderby's. "I believe it was you, unless I have had the bad luck to mistake the person in following?"

"Yes, missus," returned Stephen, "it were me."

"Have you – you'll excuse an old woman's curiosity – have you seen the gentleman?"

"Yes, missus."

"And how did he look, Sir? Was he portly, bold, outspoken, and hearty?" As she straightened her own figure, and held up her head in adapting her action to her words, the idea crossed Stephen that he had seen this old woman before, and had not quite liked her.

"O yes," he returned, observing her more attentively, "he were all that."

"And healthy," said the old woman, "as the fresh wind?"

"Yes," returned Stephen. "He were ett'n and drinking – as large and as loud as a Hummobee."

"Thank you!" said the old woman with infinite content. "Thank you!" He certainly never had seen this old woman before. Yet there was a vague remembrance in his mind, as if he has more than once dreamed of some old woman like her.

Writing about a prose extract

Here is a response that focuses hard on the question, concentrating faithfully on 'the thoughts and feelings of the reader'.

In the extract, we are with Stephen when he meets the old woman. The reader is interested to know what she is like and we are given a description of her through Stephen's thoughts, "remarking this at a glance ..." Stephen believes it is easy to understand the woman and her background, based on her appearance. Because the reader trusts Stephen's judgements, you would believe any description or opinion of her given through Stephen as fact, but this opinion may be biased. The reader is made to think that the woman is simple, because she is from the country, whereas Stephen works in Coketown. Stephen's reaction to her also makes the reader suspicious because "he had seen this old woman before, and had not quite liked her". The reader immediately wants to know what the woman did that made Stephen dislike her. The reader's curiosity is maintained as Stephen struggles with his memory. Instead of Stephen remembering why he did not like her, he is charmed by her. Her reaction to his news about Mr Bounderby seems very genuine, but the reader would still be suspicious because of Stephen's initial thoughts about her. By the end of the extract, the reader is more satisfied that the old woman is harmless. Stephen believes that "he has more than once dreamed of some old woman like her" so the reader begins to feel that she has never done anything to make him dislike her. As the chapter progresses, Stephen and the old woman walk around the town together and she remains very grateful for the information he has given her. By this point, the reader is relaxed about her being friendly towards him and no longer suspects that she has a hidden motive or that she is nasty.

Prose extracts – main task

Select an appropriate passage from the prose book you are reading and answer the following question:

* **Read the extract. Look closely at how   is presented here. How does it affect your feelings towards him/her?**

If possible, write your response 'against the clock', in the recommended time of about 20 minutes. Write about one side of A4 paper (assuming your handwriting is of average size).

Alternatively, you could answer the following question on the same extract and under the same conditions as the task above.

* **Read the extract.**
(i) **What impressions of   do you receive from this extract?**
(ii) **Choose parts of the extract you find particularly effective in creating these impressions. Write about these parts, explaining why you find them effective.**

Drama: questions for drama texts only

DRAMA has **actors**, a **director**, **stage** and **audience**. It also has **stage directions** and **sound effects** and **acts** and **scenes**. It can also have a **narrator**.

In drama, you have the added dimension of the audience. Remember, the plays you study are written to be performed in front of an audience.

Questions about the audience

> How do you think an audience would respond to this extract?

This is very similar to the reader's response for prose texts, and you need to consider the impact the extract might have on you if you were part of the audience.

Think about some or all of the following:
- Do the characters behave in typical or untypical ways? Would an audience be surprised by their behaviour?
- What do they say? How do they say it? How would this affect an audience?
- How would this extract make an audience feel? Would they feel angry? Sad? Satisfied? Excited? Happy? Shocked?
- How would an audience feel half way through the extract?
- How would an audience feel at the end of the extract?
- Would an audience's thoughts and feelings about the characters change?
- How would they change? Why would they change? When would they change?
- What specific incidents would the audience react to? Why?
- Are there stage directions and/or sound effects that would influence an audience's reaction?

Part of model answer

… I think that during this heated exchange between Eddie and Catherine the audience would be shocked. They will be amazed at the depths that Eddie will go to, to keep Catherine. The audience will start to realize that Eddie's interest in Catherine is more than just protection …

A drama extract

Read the short scene from *Under Milk Wood*, a play by Dylan Thomas about a day in the life of a rural community in Wales. The play is categorized by its writer as 'a play for voices' and started life as a radio play in the 1950s, though it has regularly featured since on stage, TV and film.

The extract follows a sample task, and a student response is provided on pages 143–4.

■ **With close reference to the extract, show how the feelings of the characters are revealed to the audience.**

Under Milk Wood – Dylan Thomas

First Voice: In the blind-drawn dark dining room of School House, dusty and echoing as a dining-room in a vault, Mr and Mrs Pugh are silent over cold grey cottage pie. Mr Pugh reads, as he forks the shroud meat in, from *Lives of the Great Poisoners*. He has bound a plain brown-paper cover round the book. Slyly, between slow mouthfuls, he sidespies up at Mrs Pugh, poisons her with his eye, then goes on reading. He underlines certain passages and smiles in secret.

Mrs Pugh: Persons with manners do not read at table,

First Voice: says Mrs Pugh. She swallows a digestive tablet as big as a horse-pill, washing it down with clouded peasoup water.

  (Pause)

Mrs Pugh: Some persons were brought up in pigsties.

Mr Pugh: Pigs don't read at table, dear.

First Voice: Bitterly she flicks dust from the broken cruet. It settles on the pie in a thin gnat-rain.

Mr Pugh: Pigs can't read, my dear.

Mrs Pugh: I know one who can.

First Voice: Alone in the hissing laboratory of his wishes, Mr Pugh minces among bad vats and jeroboams, tiptoes through spinneys of murdering herbs, agony dancing in his crucibles, and mixes especially for Mrs Pugh a venomous porridge unknown to toxicologists which will scald and viper through her until her ears fall off like figs, her toes grow big and black as balloons, and steam comes screaming out of her navel.

Mr Pugh: You know best, dear,

First Voice: Says Mr Pugh, and quick as a flash he ducks her in rat soup.

Mrs Pugh: What's that book by your trough, Mr Pugh?

Mr Pugh: It's a theological work, my dear. *Lives of the Great Saints.*

First Voice: Mrs Pugh smiles. An icicle forms in the old air of the dining vault.

Mrs Pugh: I saw you talking to a saint this morning, Saint Polly Garter. She was martyred again last night. Mrs Organ Morgan saw her with Mr Waldo.

Writing about a drama extract

Here is a response that consistently reveals an understanding of the genre of *Under Milk Wood* – the fact that this is a play and, indeed, more famously a radio play than a stage play.

It is well into the day in Llaregub, and Mr and Mrs Pugh are having a fairly depressing lunch together ('cold grey cottage pie'). It's not the first time that the audience has seen, or heard them and we know that Mr Pugh has fantasies about poisoning his wife. As First Voice says, 'he poisons her with his eye', in his dreams really, and 'smiles in secret', both of which are very detailed visual observations, reminding us that First Voice is there in the radio play to act as our eyes.

First Voice sets the scene, but the real focus of our attention is the frosty, bitter dialogue between Mr and Mrs Pugh. First Voice provides the running commentary as the husband and wife spar verbally with one another, every jibe ('Pigs can't read, my dear') matched by another ('I know one who can.').

Surprisingly, there is just one stage direction – (Pause) – but the audience would be aware of the whole exchange taking place at a slow, deliberate pace, with a tone of heavy sarcasm.

If this were to be on stage and not on radio, we would see a static scene, the Pughs sitting stiffly at a table in the middle of the stage, with the little actions exaggerated and the props highlighted. First Voice would still have a role to play, because he would draw extra attention to what was going on, as when Mrs Pugh would flick the dust from the cruet. Needless to say, all this would be very funny, if the timing was right.

Drama extracts – main task

Select an appropriate passage from the drama book you are reading and answer the following question.

♦ **Read the extract. With close reference to the text, show how the feelings of the characters are revealed to the audience.**

If possible, write your response 'against the clock', in the recommended time of about 20 minutes. Write about one side of A4 paper (assuming your handwriting is of average size).

Alternatively, you could answer the following question on the same extract and under the same conditions as the task above.

♦ **Read the extract.**

(i) **What do you think about the way _____ speaks and behaves here? Give reasons for what you say.**

(ii) **How do you think the audience would respond to this part of the play?**

Exam tips

♦ Extract questions are your best chance perhaps to show close reading skills. They are meant to be quite short, but sharp, tasks. Make sure you make key points and key references to the text in front of you.

♦ Contextualize the extract if possible, i.e. say quickly where it appears in the whole text, but do not drift into generalized discussion about the characters. Focus on the material in the extract. Your wider knowledge of the text will start to emerge anyway from your confident exploration of the extract.

♦ Try to show that you are sensitive to the genres of your texts. Therefore, *novels have readers* and *plays have audiences*.

5 English Literature

> What do you think of _____ and the way s/he is presented to the reader?
>
> What do you think is the importance of _____ to the novel as a whole?
>
> Write about the character of _____ and the way s/he is presented in the novel.
>
> Remind yourself of the ending of _____ . To what extent do you think it is a satisfactory ending?
>
> Write about the theme of _____ , showing how it is presented through different characters and how they speak and behave.
>
> To what extent do you feel sympathy for _____ ?
>
> Choose what you think is the most dramatic part of the play. Show how _____ creates dramatic tension for an audience at this point of the play.

Writing an essay in an exam is quite a difficult task, but the expectations are not unreasonable. An examination essay in literature will probably be between two and three A4 sides in length – provided you make a genuine attempt to answer an essay question with a structured, organized response based on ideas and details of the text(s) you have studied, you should do yourself justice.

Questions may focus on characters, relationships, events and themes – your aim is to respond both to the text as a whole and in some detail.

In your essay response, you should try to set a good standard in three broad areas of assessment:

1   **Knowledge and interpretation of text** – handling the text and sub-text consistently with confidence, and attempting to comment skilfully on social, historical, cultural and literary contexts
2   **Exploring language, structure and forms** – exploring and analysing the achievement of writers in creating the work of literature
3   **Conveying response** – communicating and expressing your ideas and opinions confidently and in a sustained way.

It seems right, therefore, to print a full essay response here, one done under pressure of time, to show what can be achieved in an exam. This is a fine answer to a challenging question. Above all, it is clear that it has been written by a student who has worked hard on the course and studied the set books properly. Even if this is a text that you have not studied, you should still be able to judge how much understanding of the novel is communicated to the examiner. Suffice it to say that you could show less quality and less quantity and still be proud of your efforts. On the other hand, this essay is by no means perfect (how could it be?) and you may find some points to quibble over.

The question

What impressions of country life are given in George Eliot's *Silas Marner* and how are they conveyed?

The response

George Eliot creates the images of country life all through the novel. She presents it as an idyllic place full of nature and beauty ('among the nutty hedgerows'). Country life, represented by life in Raveloe, is also shown to be a relaxed, lazy community where everything happens at a slow pace. ('orchards looking lazy with neglected plenty')

This lifestyle is contrasted heavily between the cramped, hectic life of the townspeople. This is partly how Eliot creates the image of Raveloe, by contrasting it with dark images of the town, where Silas originally came from.

The actual villagers are portrayed in an amusing way by Eliot as the reader feels that she is laughing at the inferior knowledge and simple reasoning.

Hierarchy is also very important for the village and binds the inhabitants together. They have the greatest respect for social hierarchy and believe that you cannot change your position in life.

The importance of the more wealthy characters is emphasised when Eliot describes the main house in Raveloe as 'the large red house', because this gives the impression that this family are at the top of the hierarchy as the use of the definite article makes it seem as though this house is the only large house in the village.

The hierarchy in the lower-class village is also shown when it says 'Ay, and a partic'lar thing happened, didn't it, Mr Macey?' as everyone looks up to Macey as the chief storyteller of the village, and everyone respects him.

The villagers also have a strong sense of superstition: 'And where did Master Marner get his knowledge of herbs from …'. This shows how the villagers view him as strange and different to themselves whilst reiterating their superstitious beliefs. This is shown again when it says: 'Such a sort of thing had not been known since the Wise Woman at Tarley died.' showing how basic and fundamental their medical knowledge is.

Village prejudice of anything slightly different to what they were used to is also shown: 'the parson had wanted to know what they were used to', 'the parson had wanted to know whether the peddler wore ear-rings.' as the villagers suspect him of the robbery of Silas' gold purely on the grounds that he is different 'he had a swarthy foreignness …'. The villagers dislike change and the whole village is about fifty years behind the rest of the country: 'the wine merchant's daughters from Lytherly dressed in the heights of fashion …'. This shows the old-fashioned ways of the village because no-one else dresses like these two girls and they are viewed as very fashionable, when, in fact, their style of dress was also old-fashioned which shows the double standards of life in Raveloe.

The villagers have a very relaxed view of religion. They go to church when they want and do not understand the service even when they do go. The villagers treat Christmas and other religious festivals as a huge party and not as an important time of religious significance. The villagers' simple faith is shown when Dolly says: 'it isn't to be believed as them as are above us 'ull be worse nor we are ...' They do not understand what Christianity is really about, but just accept the fact that God is good, and believe that going to church occasionally wins you a place in heaven.

The villagers have tremendous community spirit which is shown when they help Silas look for his gold, which reflects on their overall generosity.

There is great contrast between the rich and the poor in Raveloe. The rich, especially Squire Cass, are ostentatious and wasteful: '... he cut a piece of beef and held it up before the deerhound.' Whatever the rich do, however, they are still viewed as high class citizens because of the village hierarchy.

When you have read the essay, discuss the following questions:

- How well does the writer of this essay appear to know and use the text of *Silas Marner*?
- How well does the writer explore the language, the structure and the form of the novel?
- How well does the writer organize the essay and express ideas and opinions?
- Are there any constructive criticisms (either general or particular) that you would make to the writer for future literature essays?

Prose and drama: questions for both genres

Many essay tasks in drama and prose are quite similar in spirit. Both will ask you to focus on the text as a whole, but also to focus on specific features of the text. Questions may be in the following broad areas: **characters** and **relationships**, **specific events**, **endings**, **themes**.

REMEMBER Examiners are always looking for different ways to set questions, so do not become a slave to particular types of question. Remember, too, that empathy tasks (see Unit 5.3) are interchangeable with discursive essay questions in the literature exam.

Questions about characters and relationships

> What do you think is the importance of the character of _____ to the story as whole?

In answering, focus on some or all of the following:

- the speech and the behaviour of characters
- the contribution a specific character has made to the plot

- how the character interacts with others mentioned in the story and the impact this character has on the main character
- the possible consequences of the character's actions on the main plot and sub-plots of the story
- the way the character is presented to the reader and to the other characters
- any change that this character undergoes during the course of a novel or play.

Now complete the following task:
- **Choose a key character from either your prose or your drama exam text and plan in detailed note form an essay responding to the question: *What do you think is the importance of the character of   to the story as whole?***

Remember to include main ideas about the character and detailed evidence from the text.

Questions about specific events

> What is the importance of   to the story as a whole?

This kind of question asks you to focus on one specific important event in the story. When answering, think about:
- where this specific event occurs in the story – what happens just before it and what happens just after it
- the consequences of the event for the main characters in the story, how they are changed by this event and why.

You may be asked to consider 'turning points' in the story. These are events that alter a character and even change the outcome of the story.

Now complete the following task:
Choose a specific event (a key incident, scene, chapter or 'turning point') and plan in detailed note form an essay response to: *What is the importance of   to the story as a whole?*

Think about:
- the key points of the 'specific event'
- what happened to cause the event / what led to the event
- what happened as a consequence of the event to the key character(s) in the event.

Avoid simply re-telling the story.

Questions about endings

> To what extent do you think that this is a satisfactory ending?

In answering, consider the following:

- ♣ the outcome to the story in terms of how exciting or unexpected it was. Focus on the conclusion for each character and whether or not they get what they deserve. If they don't, explain how this makes the reader feel.
- ♣ how unexpected the outcome is and whether it suits the story. Think about whether the writer has given a long explanation of the ending for each character or whether the story has been concluded in a few lines.
- ♣ how the story develops to lead up to this ending.

Now complete the following task:

Choose one of your exam set texts and look at the ending of it in detail. Plan in detailed note form an essay response to the question: *To what extent do you think that this is a satisfactory ending?*

Think about:

- – the key point(s) of the final few pages or the final scene(s)
- – the outcome of the plot for the key character(s)
- – the connection (similarity/difference) with earlier situations of the key character(s)
- – the possible intentions of the writer in writing the particular ending
- – the possible reactions of the reader/audience to the ending.

Questions about themes

> Write about the ways the writer presents the theme of   in the novel.

In answering, remember that a theme in literature is a recurring idea or topic that a writer wishes to develop or repeat through the characters and action of the novel or play. The theme will be brought to life by the way the characters behave and the way the story progresses. The reader or audience will be left to interpret to their own satisfaction the clear messages coming from the novel or play. Different themes will be intertwined and some will be harder to spot than others. Revenge, loneliness, childhood, racial hatred ... are just a few of the more obvious themes that you may encounter and be required to discuss in your study of set texts.

Now complete the following task:

Choose an important theme from one of your set texts. Plan in detailed note form an essay response to the question: *Write about the ways the writer presents the theme of   in the novel.*

Think about:

- – different characters and how they speak and behave
- – different events and how they influence the theme.

Prose: questions for prose texts only

PROSE texts are divided into **chapters** and **sections**. The **narrative** will consist of **description**, **action**, **commentary** and **dialogue**.

Questions on narrative style

> Why do you think the writer chose to tell the story from the point of view of _____ ?
>
> How does the way the story is told add to the reader's enjoyment of the novel?

In answering, remember that the narrator is the storyteller of a novel or short story. There are two kinds of narrator: the one who stands outside the story as an observer and commentator –the third-person narrator; the other who is a character within the story – the first-person narrator. Every good novel and short story has a distinct narrative style. This is when the narrator actually has the 'voice' of a particular character, and the viewpoint of the narrator is restricted to the eyes and ears of that particular character.

Now complete the following task:
Look closely at the role of the narrator. Plan in detailed note form an essay response to one of the questions above.

Think about:
- the character of the narrator (what the character/narrator says and does)
- the voice of the narrator (how the narrator speaks)
- the viewpoint of the narrator (what the narrator sees and does not see)
- the way the story is organized.

Drama: questions for drama texts only

PLAYS consist of **acts** and **scenes**. The script will consist of **dialogue**, **stage directions** and **sound effects**.

Questions about dramatic technique

> Choose what you think is the most dramatic part of the play. Show how the writer creates dramatic tension for an audience.
>
> Imagine you are giving advice to someone who is going to play the part of _____ . Say how the character should be presented to an audience. If you wish, you may focus on specific parts of the play.

Although you study a play as a book, all drama comes to life on stage or screen. When tackling the above questions, you need to focus on the ways the

5 English Literature

writer adds drama to the story. Think about what happens and why, and the impact of these events on the audience. Try to relate your comments to the way the audience would think and feel while watching the play. Explore the different dramatic techniques the writer uses to make the play more interesting. Focus on what is included in the stage directions and how these instructions for sight and sound would influence the way the audience feels at a particular moment in the play. Focus on how an actor might deliver particular lines and interact with other actors/characters on stage. Remember that plays have to have drama, conflict, opposition and tension – otherwise they do not work!

Now complete the following task:

> ◆ **Choose either a scene or a character from the play you are studying. Plan in detailed note form an essay response to one of the drama questions on page 150.**

Think about:
- key lines and speeches (how they should be spoken)
- dramatic moments
- significant stage directions
- significant sound effects.

Final task

> ◆ **Choose one of the essay plans that you have made in this unit. Read it through and then write the full essay.**

If possible, write the essay 'against the clock' in the recommended time of about 40 minutes. Write two to three sides of A4 paper (assuming your handwriting is of average size).

Exam tips

- ◆ Always do your best to answer the question set. Do not answer the question you were hoping to get or the one that you answered in the 'mock' exam!
- ◆ Be cool under pressure and start your response thoughtfully. Make your opening sentences and opening paragraph meaningful, make definite points and win the confidence of the examiner.
- ◆ Think in terms of overview and detail. Show that you are in touch with the writer's ideas and that also you know different parts of the text well enough to impress.
- ◆ Revise intelligently. Even if you do not write many practice essays, do make sure that you think through possible questions and how you would deal with them. Work out a coherent position on as many questions as possible, so that you can start an essay response with some purpose.

Unit 5.3 Empathy questions

When answering empathy questions you need to imagine you are a given character. You must 'put yourself in their shoes' and write in ways that are typical of that character, using words and phrases that they might use.

In simple terms, the key to empathy tasks is to write in the first person. This means you would expect to use 'I', 'me' and 'my' from the standpoint of your character.

Refer to events or to conversations that your character participated in. Try not to refer to any events that the character would not be aware of.

Exploring character

Empathy questions on both prose and drama texts will ask you to imagine you are a specific character from the text. Begin by writing in the **first person**. You need to concentrate hard to ensure you maintain the use of 'I' and 'me' throughout your answer.

In your response you should **explore character**. Try to explain your character's thoughts and feelings as if they are your own. Reflect on the events of the text – those that involve your character and others. Make a particular effort to explain the events that led up to the conclusion of the story. You should also explore and explain your relationships with other characters and your reactions to what they say and do. You also need to explain the reasons for your behaviour throughout the text.

Part of model answer
... It could perhaps be said that racism is socially accepted in Maycomb County and this is the main reason why Tom was convicted. Although many people didn't agree with my actions I just wouldn't have been able to hold my head up high on the streets if I had not defended an innocent man, despised because of the colour of his skin ...

Now complete the following task:

♠ **Choose a character from either your prescribed prose text or your prescribed drama text and write a few original lines spoken by that character to reveal an aspect of their personality.**

Adopting the character's speech patterns

When writing as a specific character, you should try to adopt their **way of speaking**, and possibly their **dialect** and any **distinctive words** they use. This might mean using the same slang terms as that character and the same 'pet' names for the other characters in the text. For example, Paddy Clarke (in *Paddy Clarke Ha Ha Ha*) calls his father 'Da' rather than 'Daddy', 'Pa' or 'Pop'. It is surprising how much one or two authentic touches can add to your writing, making it seem more realistic and believable. For example, in *To Kill a Mockingbird* do Scout and Jem call Boo Radley 'Boo' or 'Mr Radley'? With characters from Shakespeare, you have to try to create the effect of a speech style, without resorting to Shakespearean verse.

> **Part of model answer**
>
> ... I return to my father, Prospero, whose dukedom was unknown to me until the day when, using his magical art, he caused a terrible tempest to arise from nowhere, which seemingly destroyed a passing boat (though I later learned that this was a further example of his power, as the boat was miraculously restored before the day was done).

Now complete the following task:

♠ **Choose another character from one of your prescribed texts and write just two or three sentences that imitate their voice.**

Using quotations

Quotation is quite difficult to achieve in an empathy response, but you should aim to 'echo' the words of the text. There are some particular difficulties that prevent neat use of the text within a character's stream of consciousness, but keep a look out for possibilities and build the skill into your practice. Start with words and short phrases and generally do not quote at excessive length. Try to parallel the high level skill of integrating quotations into a traditional essay. In an empathy response, however, you do not need to use quotation marks, unless, of course, you are quoting another character or quoting yourself from another occasion.

Part of model answer

... I often got fed up of Lennie but I loved him. I always got frustrated at him when he was so forgetful, I hadda repeat myself several times, and Lennie always being so apologetic all the time. Though Lennie, he listened to me and he did remember 'the dream'. That was one thing he would never forget. The rabbits and to live off the 'fatta the lan'...

Now complete the following task:

- **Choose another character from a set text and weave words from the text into a short sequence of your character's thoughts and feelings.**

Arthur Miller's play *A View From The Bridge* deals with the troubled life of Eddie Carbone, a New York docker. He and his wife, Beatrice, give shelter in their tenement flat to Beatrice's Italian cousins, who are illegal immigrants. Catherine, Beatrice's niece, who has been brought up by Beatrice and Eddie, falls in love with one of them …

Here are extracts of an answer to the following question. It empathizes with Alfieri, a key Italian-American character in the play. Alfieri is a Brooklyn lawyer and effectively the narrator of the play.

- **Imagine you are Alfieri. Write down your thoughts and feelings at the end of the play.**

When Eddie first arrived at my office, I immediately sensed that he was unhappy. I had always suspected that his feelings for Catherine ran much deeper than ordinary guardian love, but it was not my place to express these suspicions. However, after that doomed day, Eddie abandoned all other hopes and committed the ultimate betrayal. However much I convince myself that I was powerless to prevent him, I often wonder if an alternative action on my behalf would have resulted in Eddie's live presence today …

… I can recall the advice that I gave to Eddie on our first meeting, and I almost allowed my suspicions to speak for me. I remember saying: "She wants to get married … she can't marry you, can she?" Eddie's reaction was one of unbelievable shock and denial, and it was at that precise moment I realised how complicated the situation had become. He exited from my office a troubled man …

… The arrival of the immigration officer shocked Beatrice and Catherine, but still Eddie remained in denial of his actions. Marco suddenly became very protective of his younger brother and accused Eddie of calling the Immigration Bureau. I had to give Marco advice on how to deal with Eddie; I warned him not to seek revenge, despite how he felt towards the man. Marco was not willing to accept my advice, I could see that in his eyes, but he promised to steer clear of trouble …

… I suppose the ending of the story was meant to be. Eddie was such an emotionally unstable man that he would never be content with his life …

This has many ingredients of a high-level empathy response. It reveals deep understanding of the characters from Alfieri's standpoint, which is partly the detached, intelligent outsider but also the knowing, sympathetic insider. He understands the motivations of the characters and his 'voice' is entirely convincing. This answer (even in this much shortened form) touches several of the play's themes and explores the issue of guilt. There is a deadpan, tired quality in the presentation of Alfieri here, which is in keeping with how the character would be at the end of the play, reflecting on the action.

Choose a character from one of your prescribed texts and attempt a full empathy response to the question:

🔹 **Imagine you are   . At the end of the story you think back over what has happened. Write your thoughts and feelings. Remember how   would speak when you write your answer.**

Write the essay 'against the clock' in the recommended time of about 40 minutes. Write two to three sides of A4 paper (assuming your handwriting is of average size).

You may wish to think about:
— the events leading up to the conclusion of the story
— your relationships with the other characters.

Exam tips

🔹 Put yourself in the shoes of the named character at the point where s/he is looking back at events. Work out the key qualities of the character and emphasize them throughout your response.

🔹 Select the key parts of the action, those that would be 'on the mind' of your character. Don't allow yourself to lapse into a flat, uninteresting re-telling of the story.

🔹 Enrich the 'voice' of your character with a sense of the speech patterns or quirks of vocabulary and style that give some individuality.

🔹 Incorporate the original text by echoes of the words actually spoken or in some cases even using quotations, those words and phrases that the character might naturally recall.

Unit 5.4 Poetry appreciation

> Write about the poem and its effect on you.
>
> You may wish to include some or all of these points:
> - the poem's content – what it is about
> - the ideas the poet may have wanted us to think about
> - the mood or atmosphere of the poem
> - how it is written – words or phrases you find interesting, the way the poem is structured or organized, and so on
> - your response to the poem.

An **unseen poem** is so called because when you face it in an exam, the chances are that you will be seeing it for the first time. In other words, it is a *previously* unseen poem, one that you have not revised or studied, unless you are very lucky. Everyone sitting the examination will experience the same feeling of unease with a new text, so do not panic. See this as nothing more than a test of your reading skills, in much the same way as you face the literary prose extracts in the English exam (covered in Section 1 of this book). There will be no tricks in the question. You will be required to write about the poem and its effect on you – nothing more, nothing less.

When you first see the 'unseen poem', read it through carefully. Then carefully re-read the question you have been given and each of the bullet points. Then read through the poem a second time, considering as you read what you will write for each of the bullet points. You may also be given a line or two of information about the poem. Do not ignore it.

The key to unseen poetry tasks is not to panic if you think you do not understand the poem. It is perfectly acceptable to write that the poem is 'confusing' or 'misleading' in your response, if you can specify where the difficulty lies. You may be on to something important. Do not, however, make the general admission: 'At first I found the poem difficult, but I gradually found it easier to understand.' That should be true of every poem.

Concentrate on exactly what is being asked of you. This means treating the poem as a whole, considering each of the bullet points, and thinking about how the poem makes you feel and what you think as you read it.

Read the poem 'Laugharne Castle' by John Idris Jones. The poet looks thoughtfully at the ancient castle as it stands now in the present day. (Laugharne is a small town on Camarthen Bay in south-west Wales. Richard Hughes and Dylan Thomas are well-known writers from Wales, and they both lived close to Laugharne Castle.)

LAUGHARNE CASTLE –

John Idris Jones

Against the cliff
like curtains
left after a play
brown as mud, holed, ivied, roofless,
a straggled jetsam.

Between the houses of
Richard Hughes and Dylan Thomas,
surviving despite weather and neglect
without improvement or attention or adulation,
it writes its own history.

Curlews call,
shoulders of mud glisten,
the sea swings, takes, changes,
moving sand, river and shore.

The castle remains
against the rocking and ooze of tides:
an eye and a hand
watching,
representing.

Now write a full answer to the following question:

> **Write about the poem and its effect on you.**

Before you start, complete a grid like the one below, focusing on each of the bullet points in your response. By doing this you will cover the main points about the poem.

BULLET POINT	COMMENT
The poem's content *Add a comment of your own about each of the four sections of the poem. Use your own words to describe the castle, echoing the thoughts and feelings of the poet.*	*The castle stands on the coast, apparently abandoned.*
The ideas the poet may have wanted us to think about *Add two or three sentences to the one on the right. Create your comments from a close reading of the poem.*	*The poet sets us thinking about history and the passing of time.*
The mood or atmosphere of the poem *Write two or three sentences about the mood or atmosphere, building on the first sentence on the right and moving towards the end of the poem.*	*At first the castle seems forlorn and crumbling.* *At the end of the poem, the castle has the strength to survive.*
Words or phrases you find interesting *Choose three examples of interesting use of language and comment on them.*	*'a straggled jetsam'*
The way the poem is structured or organized *Comment on how the poem develops from beginning to end, and, if you can, comment on the separate meaning of the four distinct parts.*	
Your response to the poem *End with two or three comments of 'personal response', drawing out any last comments of understanding and appreciation.*	

Cameraman

Sheenagh Pugh

You must see all suffering,
all cruelty, all injustice, all pain:
you must fix your eye on the starving,
the tortured and the executed: you
must look away from nothing.
You must not turn your hand
to feed the children, nor to caress
the dying, nor to defend
victims. You keep the lens
in front of your mind,
that others may reach
into pockets, knock on doors,
dig wells. You are the itch
in others; you can make them
see clear; if only you watch
exactly; if you record
just what happened. Do not be tempted
to turn the camera inward:
your stricken looks are no concern
of the public's. They need the word
not what you saw, not how
you felt. It is they who must feel
they saw it; they were there; so
involved, they condemned somewhat
the remote likes of you.

Now answer the following question:

    ❖   **Write about the poem and its effect on you.**

Think about who is speaking to whom. Is the voice accusing, sympathetic, puzzled, troubled?

How do you think a news cameraman can cope with the circumstances of his (or her) work?

Before you start writing, complete a grid like the one below. This will help you prepare comments for a full response to the poem

BULLET POINT	COMMENT
■ The poem's content	
■ Ideas the poet may have wanted us to think about	
■ The mood or atmosphere of the poem	
■ Words or phrases you find interesting	
■ The way the poem is structured or organized	
■ Your response to the poem	

Read the poem 'Home' by Rupert Brooke. The speaker (or persona) relates a simple tale that might be explained in a number of ways, depending on your beliefs.

Home –

Rupert Brooke

I came back late and tired last night
Into my little room,
To the long chair and the firelight
And comfortable gloom.

But as I entered softly in
I saw a woman there,
The line of neck and cheek and chin,
The darkness of her hair,
The form of one I did not know
Sitting in my chair.

I stood a moment fierce and still,
Watching her neck and hair,
I made a step to her; and saw
That there was no one there.

It was some trick of the firelight
That made me see her there.
It was a chance of shade and light
And the cushion in the chair.

Oh, all you happy over the earth,
That night, how could I sleep?
I lay and watched the lonely gloom;
And watched the moonlight creep
From wall to basin, round the room.
All night I could not sleep.

Now answer the question:

* **Write about the poem and its effect on you.**

Think carefully about the poem, including its title, before you write your answer. Explore the situation in some depth and consider the man's personality sympathetically.

Below is the beginning of a possible answer. Either continue this response to give a full answer or start again.

The man in the poem seems to live a life of solitude. He sits in the dark in his room and does not have many possessions around him. 'The comfortable gloom' suggests that his home offers him warmth and comfort, but little to inspire him. He imagines that he has some company, in the form of a woman sitting in his chair beside the fire … He perhaps blames the vision that he sees on the fact that he arrived home 'late and tired' …

Read the poem 'Song' by W.H. Auden, in which the poet observes what 'Love' can do to people.

Song – W. H. Auden

> The chimney sweepers
> Wash their faces and forget to wash the neck
> The lighthouse keepers
> Let the lamps go out and leave the ships to wreck;
> The prosperous baker
> Leaves the rolls in hundreds in the oven to burn;
> The undertaker
> Pins a small note on the coffin saying "Wait till I return,
> I've got a date with Love."
>
> And deep-sea divers
> Cut their boots off and come bubbling to the top,
> And engine-drivers
> Bring expresses in the tunnel to a stop;
> The village rector
> Dashes down the side-aisle half-way through a psalm;
> The sanitary inspector
> Runs off with the cover of the cesspool on his arm –
> To keep his date with Love.

Now answer the following question:

♠ **Write about the poem and its effect on you.**

Spend about 30 minutes on this task and write between one and one-and-a-half sides of A4 paper, treating it as an exam question. Think carefully about the poem, including its title, before you write your answer.

You may wish to include some or all of these points:
♠ the poem's content – what it is about
♠ the ideas the poet may have wanted us to think about
♠ the mood or atmosphere of the poem
♠ how it is written – words or phrases you find interesting, the way the poem is structured or organized, and so on
♠ your response to the poem.

Exam tips

♠ You do not need to give a particularly long response to the poem, so it is valuable to read the poem thoughtfully for quite a few minutes before you start writing your answer. Your first writing should really take the form of a set of annotations around the poem on the question paper.
♠ Do not write comments about technical terms that have no relevance to the meaning of the poem. If one of your comments means nothing, it will be worth nothing.
♠ Keep quotations short and weave them into your writing for best effect. Choose the words and phrases that stand out as worthy of comment.

5 English Literature

English Literature (Specification B)

Anthology comparison tasks (prose and poetry)

Compare the endings of any **two** stories in the anthology. As a general guide, you might like to look at the last 30 lines of each story.

Some of these stories are about important incidents in childhood, which may have been painful for the child involved. Compare **two** that are about childhood.

Most of the poems you have studied are about people. Choose **two** poems about people, which have made a particular impact on you, and write about them.

Choose **two poems by different poets** where the poet has used imagery that you find particularly effective. Write about them, explaining how the imagery has added to your understanding and enjoyment.

Clear-minded **organization** is the most important ingredient of an answer to a **comparison** task on literature. You need a firm direction from the start of your answer and this will only come from conscientious revision, a confident approach to comparison, and quick-witted planning on the day.

You need to know the value of the things you might decide to compare – stick to meaningful comparisons, avoiding things that have little or no bearing on an understanding of the text(s). Avoid counting words and spotting alliteration!

Two texts (or characters) may have **identical features** on the one hand or they may be diametrically **opposite** to each other, but it is just as likely that they have **close and not-so-close similarities** and that they have both **sharp and more subtle differences**. Always remember that no author writes with the primary intention that you compare his or her work with something else! Do not try to make a work of literature fit a template or formula just to suit the drift of your response.

The essay openings and conclusions on the following pages show how the skilful balancing of points and comments can give great authority to a 'comparison' response. However, it is also necessary to write in a sustained way about each of the two (or three) texts that you are comparing. Avoid a ping-pong essay structure where you switch time and time again from one text to the other and never settle to say anything substantial about each one. Try to sustain the discussion on each of the texts and make the connections where they do not seem forced and artificial.

Prose comparison

Consider

openings   setting   action   characters   narrators

endings   skills   ideas   periods   personal responses

The PROSE anthology comparison task requires you to write about two of the prose extracts from the anthology. You may have a free choice for the prose you write about or the two pieces may be given in the question.

The key to the prose anthology task is to discuss the two pieces of prose in a balanced way. Present the same information about each of the two texts, including:

* what the pieces are about
* how they are different and similar
* why you find each piece interesting.

An essay opening

Snowdrops and *Extraordinary Little Cough* are two short stories which both focus upon painful experiences during childhood. *Snowdrops* is about a young boy who has to face the reality of adulthood and how painful it can be. *Extraordinary Little Cough* is about a boy called George who is an outcast which proves to be a painful experience for him.

A similarity between the two stories is that both the boys experience restrictions imposed upon them by adults. The boy in *Snowdrops* is enthralled by the snowdrops but couldn't see them because he is prevented by adults. The image of the snowdrops being somewhere he was not allowed to go is symbolic of the restrictions placed upon children by adults throughout their childhood ('where they weren't allowed to go'). Similarly, in *Extraordinary Little Cough*, George is clearly victimized as a result of the way in which his mother restricts him. His mother gives him a different bag to all his friends which makes him look foolish. Due to the protective nature of his mother, he is also less experienced than his friends, another reason for him being victimized ('But George had never left home for more than one night.') ...

Questions about characters

Choose two characters, each from different stories, with whom you felt involved. Compare the characters, and explain why you felt involved with them.

Select characters that you can write plenty about. Do not write about characters that only appear for one or two lines or do not say or do anything interesting. You could pick characters you either really like or really dislike because this will give you the opportunity to explain how the writer makes you feel involved with them.

In answering, consider the following:
- how the characters are presented
- how the characters speak and behave – both when alone and when with the other characters
- the characters' thoughts and feelings and how these change
- how the characters change and/or develop through the story
- how your thoughts and feelings change towards the characters
- what causes your thoughts and feelings to change
- how others react towards this character
- whether the story is written in the first person (giving a biased view of the characters) or written in the third person (possibly a more objective view of the characters).

Now complete the following task:

Write an opening paragraph (or two) in response to the question:
Choose two characters, each from different stories in the anthology, with whom you felt involved. Compare the characters, and explain why you felt involved with them.

Questions about relationships

> …Select two of these stories [in the anthology] and compare the impressions the writers give of parent–child relationships.

You need to have a good understanding of the relationships in the stories and be able to identify immediately which ones discuss the same types of relationship – for example, parent/child, male/female, teacher/student.

When answering, you could also focus on:
- how the relationships are presented
- how the characters in the relationships speak and behave towards each other – both in public and in private
- the characters' thoughts and feelings towards their relationships and how these change
- how the relationships change and/or develop during the story
- how your thoughts and feelings change towards the characters' relationships
- what causes your thoughts and feelings to change
- how other characters react towards the relationships.

Now complete the following task:
- **Write the opening paragraph (or two) in response to the question above about parent–child relationships.**

Compare two stories about childhood.

Before attempting this question you need to identify the stories that share a similar theme and explore what exactly that theme is. Then you could consider each of the following points:

- how the writers convey that theme through their stories
- why the writers have chosen to convey this message
- the literary techniques used to enhance the reader's understanding of the theme
- the similarities and differences between the stories
- the intended effect of each story on the reader
- how this effect is created
- how your thoughts and feelings change as you read each story
- why your thoughts and feelings change.

Now complete the following task:

- **Write the opening paragraph (or two) in response to the question above on the theme of childhood.**

Questions about endings

Compare the endings of any two stories in the anthology.

If you are given a free choice for the two stories, then pick two endings that you find particularly memorable or that you particularly liked or disliked. Again, this will give you plenty to comment on while writing your response.

In answering, respond to each of the following points:

- how the writers build up to their conclusion
- whether the conclusion is long and detailed or summed up in a few short lines
- how unexpected or exciting the ending is
- what happens to each character at the end of the story
- whether each character gets what they deserve or not
- your thoughts and feelings about the outcome for each character and how these feelings are created
- whether the ending suits the rest of the story
- whether the ending influences your thoughts and feelings about the rest of the story
- whether any devices have been used, such as flashbacks, cliff-hangers or twists.

Now complete the following task:

- **Write an opening paragraph (or two) in response to the above question about story endings.**

An essay conclusion

... In conclusion, despite the age gap between the children in the stories, the characters are very similar. This shows that as you grow older it doesn't make it any easier to cope with traumatic experiences.

Prose comparison: final task

* **Choose the two stories that you have enjoyed most from the WJEC anthology. Write about what it is that you enjoyed about each of them. Look for the particular points of interest in each story and the way each story is written. Avoid a straight re-telling of the stories.**

Write the essay 'against the clock' in the recommended time of about 40 minutes. Write two to three sides of A4 paper (assuming your handwriting is of average size).

You may wish to think about:
– what they are about
– how they are written
– how they are alike and how they are different
– anything else you think important.

Poetry comparison

Consider
themes moods settings types styles periods structures narratives viewpoints personal responses

The POETRY anthology comparison task will generally require you to write about two poems from the anthology. Depending on the question, you may select the poems or they may be chosen for you. If you have a free choice for the poems, select two of comparable length that you think you can write a convincing essay about.

Please note that 'School at Four O'Clock' by Charles Causley is not included in the 2005–2007 WJEC anthology.

An essay opening

Both 'School at Four O'Clock' and 'In Mrs Tilscher's Class' are written from the poets' experiences. They have similar messages of how school cannot help students, although Charles Causley is much more negative about it and feels school is useless while Carol Ann Duffy only thinks that Mrs Tilscher cannot help the children when they reach their adolescence ...

Questions about the poems of one writer

> Write about two of _____'s poems that made a particular impact on you.

The main thing is to only write about **two** poems by the given writer. Do exactly as the question instructs and you cannot go far wrong in your response. Cover both of the poems equally and consider the following:

♣ what the two poems are about
♣ who the speakers are in the poems
♣ what the poems have in common and how they differ
♣ the way each poem is written
♣ the effects the poems have on you, in terms of how your thoughts and feelings change as you read them
♣ how these poems create these effects on you.

Now complete the following task:

♣ **Write the opening paragraph (or two) of a response to the above question on two poems by the same poet.**

Questions about poetic technique

> Choose two poems by different poets where the poet has used an effective poetic technique. How effective do you find the use of the technique(s)? What impact does it / do they have on you, and why?

You need to have a full understanding of the different poetic techniques used in the poems in the anthology before you enter the exam. For example, you could be asked about imagery or first-person 'narrative' or colloquialisms used in the poems.

In answering a question of this type, you could focus on the following points:

♣ how the poetic techniques are used in **two poems**
♣ the effect that these poetic techniques have on the content of the poems
♣ how your thoughts and feelings change towards the content or theme of the poems because of the use of these poetic techniques
♣ why your thoughts and feelings change
♣ how the poetic techniques influence your understanding of the poems
♣ the intended impact of these techniques on the reader.

Now complete the following task:

♣ **Write an opening paragraph (or two) in response to the question above on poetic technique.**

Questions about themes

> Several of the poems you have studied share a theme. Choose two poems on the same theme and write about them.

Before attempting this question you need to identify the poems that share a similar theme and explore what exactly that theme is. Then you could consider each of the following points:

- ♣ how the writers convey that theme through their poems
- ♣ why the writers have chosen to convey this message
- ♣ the poetic techniques used to enhance the reader's understanding of the theme
- ♣ the similarities and differences between the poems
- ♣ the intended effect of each poem on the reader
- ♣ how this effect is created
- ♣ your thoughts and feelings as you read each poem.

Now complete the following task:

- ♣ **Write an opening paragraph (or two) in response to the question above on a shared theme. Introduce your two poems and the theme that they share.**

An essay conclusion

… Carol Ann Duffy ends with a strong image 'thunderstorm', which represents the turbulence of adolescence that is ahead and how school cannot prepare you for it. Charles Causley's last statement is also extremely powerful: 'And were not fed'. It sums up his view of the education system and how children yearn to be taught, but aren't, and reflects his views as a teacher himself.

Both of these poems highlight what is lacking in the education system, although Carol Ann Duffy gives a more balanced view, showing what positive experiences she had in school as well as the negative.

Poetry comparison: final task

- ♣ **Choose your two favourite poems from the WJEC anthology. (Your choices should represent two poets.) Write about what it is about each one that made an impact on you.**

Write the essay 'against the clock' in the recommended time of about 40 minutes. Write two to three sides of A4 paper.

You may wish to think about:

- – what the poems are about
- – what their messages are
- – the way they are written
- – how they are alike and how they are different
- – why they made an impact on you
- – anything else you think important.

- In Specification B, as elsewhere, your personal response will be valued. Try to engage with the stories and poems of the anthology and respond honestly, but sensitively, to the characters, events and themes.

- Try to show some appreciative understanding of the way the poems and stories have been written – particular approaches and styles in whole texts and particularly effective details (key words, phrases and sentences). Do not off-load irrelevant technical terms – if one or two fit naturally into your writing as part of your personal response, use them but otherwise leave well alone!

- Organization is the key to effective comparison, but do not go overboard with an unnecessarily large number of comparisons. If one poem or story makes you sad, and another makes you angry, this is an important comparison (or contrast) that needs developing on both sides. Make sure that you write clearly and effectively on each individual text.

English exams (Papers 1 and 2)

English exam papers 1 and 2 are worth 30% each of the overall marks. In both papers you are assessed in reading and writing – see the following pages for full outlines.

Tips

Revise for English by practising your skills on specimen questions and papers.

Do some preparation 'against the clock', especially testing your writing accuracy under pressure.

Learn to look for the key words in questions and instructions.

English Literature exam (Specifications A and B)

This exam is worth 70% of the marks in English Literature.

Tips

Tackle the subject properly – get involved in your set books by reading them at home.

Have some confidence in your own thoughts and back them up with evidence from the text – don't off-load your teacher's notes.

Learn to answer the questions – don't just re-tell the story.

REMEMBER

Think before you write and check your work when you finish.

Show that you are in control of what you are doing and that you know when to stop.

Written coursework (English and English Literature)

Coursework counts for 20% of your marks in English and 30% in English Literature. You will need four pieces for English and four for English Literature, but because of overlaps between the subjects you may only need six pieces overall – see the WJEC Coursework Guide, also published by Oxford University Press, for details.

Tips

Do your very best on each piece from the very start of the course – this will save you time later.

Take advice, but don't be too dependent on your teacher – you'll be on your own in the exams.

Speaking & listening

Speaking and listening is worth 20% of the marks in English. You will be assessed by your teacher throughout the course, but there will be a focus on three specific tasks done in class.

Tips

Be positive about all of your day-to-day classroom activities in English.

Have a real go at the assessment tasks – work on improving your skills.

WJEC ENGLISH

GCSE PAPER 1

(2 hours)

Foundation and Higher Tiers

Section A (about 55 minutes recommended)

Reading

Answer *four* questions on a prose extract

| A1 | 10 marks | 10–15 minutes |

| A2 | 10 marks | 10–15 minutes |

| A3 | 10 marks | 10–15 minutes |

| A4 | 10 marks | 10–15 minutes |

Note: Sometimes one 10 mark question will be replaced by two worth 5 marks each.

(Questions test: knowledge and use of text; inference and interpretation; appreciation and evaluation of language and structure.)

Section B (about 1 hour 5 minutes recommended)

Writing

Complete *two* pieces of writing

| B1 | 20 marks | 25 minutes approximately |

Descriptive writing

| B2 | 20 marks | 40 minutes approximately |

Imaginative writing

(Writing assessed on: content and organization; sentence structure, punctuation and spelling.)

WJEC ENGLISH

GCSE PAPER 2

Foundation and Higher Tiers

(2 hours)

Section A (about 50 minutes recommended)

Reading

Answer a total of *four* questions on a non-fiction text and a media text

A1	10 marks	10–15 minutes
A2	10 marks	10–15 minutes
A3	10 marks	10–15 minutes
A4	10 marks	10–15 minutes

Note: Sometimes one 10 mark question will be replaced by two worth 5 marks each.

(Questions test: knowledge and use of text, including cross-referencing; inference and interpretation; appreciation and evaluation of language, structure and presentation.)

Section B (about 1 hour 10 minutes recommended)

Writing

Complete *two* pieces of writing

B1   20 marks   35 minutes approximately

Transactional/discursive writing

B2   20 marks   35 minutes approximately

Transactional/discursive writing

(Writing assessed on: content and organization; sentence structure, punctuation and spelling.)

GCSE ENGLISH LITERATURE

SPECIFICATION A
Written Paper

(2 hours 30 minutes)

Foundation and Higher Tiers

Section A (about one hour recommended)

Prose

Close reading of extract from set text	10 marks	20 minutes
Extended writing on set text	20 marks	40 minutes

Section B (about one hour recommended)

Drama

Close reading of extract from set text	10 marks	20 minutes
Extended writing on set text	20 marks	40 minutes

Section C (about 30 minutes)

Guided response to unseen poem	10 marks	30 minutes

(Questions test: knowledge and interpretation of text; exploration of language, structure and forms; conveying response; relating texts to their social, cultural and historical contexts and literary traditions, as relevant.)

WJEC
CBAC

GCSE ENGLISH LITERATURE

SPECIFICATION B (Anthology)
Written Paper

(2 hours 30 minutes)

Foundation and Higher Tiers

Section A

Prose Anthology (about 55 minutes recommended)

Close reading of extract from anthology	10 marks	about 15 minutes
Extended writing on anthology	20 marks	about 40 minutes

Section B

Poetry Anthology (about 55 minutes recommended)

Close reading of extract from anthology	10 marks	about 15 minutes
Extended writing on anthology	20 marks	about 40 minutes

Section C (about 40 minutes)

Drama

Extended writing on set text	20 marks	about 40 minutes

(Questions test: knowledge and interpretation of text; exploration of language, structure and forms; conveying response; making comparisons; relating texts to their social, cultural and historical contexts and literary traditions, as relevant.)